MW01123998

Cajun Cooking
Southern Style

Cajun Cooking
Southern Style

FIVE
GENERATIONS
OF
FAMILY
RECIPES

Pat Saizan Corbin

HILLSBORO PRESS
Franklin, Tennessee

Printed in the United States of America

04   03   02   01   00   1   2   3   4   5

Library of Congress Catalog Card Number: 00-107570

ISBN: 1-57736-206-3

Cover design by Gary Bozeman

Cover photos clockwise from top left: Chantelle Prejean's first crabbing trip; Louisiana crab boil; sisters, Shirley Micelli and Lurline Duplechain preparing food; brothers John and Caleb Corbin show off a largemouth bass; Gulf Coast shrimp boats; Charlotte Saizan cuts into a birthday cake. Pat Saizan and cousin Richie Thibodeaux look on.

Recipe Consultant: Shirley Burger Jones

HILLSBORO PRESS
PROVIDENCE HOUSE PUBLISHERS

238 Seaboard Lane • Franklin, Tennessee 37067
800-321-5692
www.providencehouse.com

TO MY FATHER

JIM SAIZAN

AND ALL OTHER GREAT COOKS
PAST AND PRESENT

*C*ontents

Preface & Acknowledgments

LOUISIANA—A SPORTSMAN'S PARADISE! NOWHERE ELSE in the world can you catch your supper from your front-yard ditch. What a wonderful place to grow up with such an abundance of wildlife, seafood, and water sports. You don't realize how lucky you are until you move away.

Shortly after I moved to Tennessee, my father passed away. It was after his death that I realized I had to preserve the family history by compiling a Cajun cookbook. What a wonderful legacy to record and pass on.

I am a descendant of both Cajun and Creole ancestry. My father's name, Saizan, is French, and his mother's name, Rodrigue, is Portuguese. Both were early Louisiana settlers. The Acadian influx began in 1713 when a refugee ship landed in New Orleans with five thousand people on board. The Cajuns were simple, happy people who lived off the land and created their own style of spicy country cooking.

In 1763, the Spanish began arriving. They were referred to as Criolla, which later changed to Creole. Their cooking was an elegant, more sophisticated style of city cooking.

This cookbook is a collection of wonderful recipes from at least five generations of my family, with many recipes that are over one hundred years old as well as newer family favorites. It represents Cajun, Creole, Spanish, Indian, African, and Southern cooking.

Growing up in Louisiana was such a wonderful experience with such a diverse "melting pot" of foods. It has been my pleasure to collect these recipes and carry on these memories.

Special thanks to Lurline Rodrigue Duplechain for all her research and recipe contributions; to my mother, Charlotte Sundberg Saizan; my daughters, Cara Corbin Burleson and Aimee Corbin; and my friend Mary Parton, for their help and recipe experimentations; and to my husband, John Corbin, for his computer artwork. And thanks to all other family and friends for their recipes, picture contributions, and tolerance for all those tested recipes!

*A*ppetizers & *B*everages

APPETIZERS

Garfish Balls 4 • Shrimp Balls 4 • Homemade Cocktail Sauce 5 • Shrimp and Rice Fritters 5 • Potato Crab Cakes 6 • Traditional Crab Cakes 6 • Cajun Seasoning 7 • Cheesy Crab Dip 7 • Crawfish Remoulade 8 • Crawfish Balls 9 • Black-eyed Pea Salsa 9 • Favorite Shrimp Mold 10 • Mama's Shrimp Dip 10 • Praline Fruit Dip 11 • Pineapple Cheese Ball 11 • Cheese and Pecan Wafers 12 • Shrimp Puffs 12 • Crab-Stuffed Banana Peppers 13 • Fried Cheese Bites 13 • Cajun Crackers 14 • Stuffed Mushrooms 14 • Oysters on the Half Shell 15 • Meatballs Piquant 15 • Piquant Sauce 16

BEVERAGES

Holiday Punch 16 • Spiced Cinnamon Tea 16 • Spiced Apple Cider 17 • Fruit Tea 17 • Grandma's Lemonade 17 • Nearly Beer Coffee 18 • Choco Coffee 18 • Café Royale 18 • Café au Lait 19 • Café Rhum 19 • Coffee Punch 19

Center photo: This garfish was caught by Fletcher Corbin, son of a Methodist minister, sometime in the 1920s in Alabama. For an excellent garfish recipe, see Garfish Balls on page 4.

Clockwise from left to right: Gulf Coast shrimp boats. My father, Jim Saizan. Sisters Shirley Micelli and Lurline Duplechain preparing food. Maque choux or fried corn. Chantelle Prejean's first crabbing trip. Louisiana crab boil. Brothers Caleb and John Corbin show off a largemouth bass.

Garfish Balls

1	POUND GARFISH OR ANY FISH, DEBONED
$1/2$	CUP ONION, CHOPPED
$1/4$	CUP CELERY, CHOPPED
1	EGG, BEATEN
$1/2$	CUP SEASONED BREAD CRUMBS, DIVIDED
1	TABLESPOON PARSLEY FLAKES
$1/2$	TEASPOON CAJUN SEASONING
	OIL FOR FRYING

In a food processor or meat grinder, blend raw garfish and vegetables together. Transfer to a mixing bowl and add remaining ingredients, reserving $1/4$ cup seasoned bread crumbs. Mix well. With a teaspoon, scoop up spoonfuls and mold into balls, about one inch in size. Roll in reserved bread crumbs and fry in one-inch deep hot oil until golden brown. Drain and serve with ketchup or Homemade Cocktail Sauce, (see p. 5). Yield: 24 1-inch balls.

The garfish is said to date back to the dinosaur days. Today there are several species of garfish found in all types of water. One species called the "alligator gar," can grow up to ten-feet long and is found predominantly in the southern United States.

Shrimp Balls

1	POUND SHRIMP, PEELED AND DEVEINED
1	EGG, BEATEN
$1/2$	CUP SEASONED BREAD CRUMBS, DIVIDED
$1/4$	CUP CELERY
$1/4$	CUP ONION, FINELY CHOPPED
1	TABLESPOON PARSLEY FLAKES
$1/2$	TEASPOON CAJUN SEASONING
	OIL FOR FRYING

Grind or chop raw shrimp. Set aside. In a mixing bowl, soak $1/4$ cup bread crumbs in egg. Add remaining ingredients, mixing well. With a teaspoon, scoop up spoonfuls and mold into balls about one inch in size. Roll in reserved bread crumbs and fry in one-inch deep hot oil until golden brown. Drain and serve plain or with Homemade Cocktail Sauce, (see p. 5). Yield: 24 balls.

Homemade Cocktail Sauce

$1^1/_2$ CUPS KETCHUP
$^1/_4$ CUP LEMON JUICE
2 TABLESPOONS PREPARED HORSERADISH
1 TABLESPOON PLUS 1 TEASPOON WORCESTERSHIRE SAUCE
1 TEASPOON ONION, FINELY CHOPPED
   RED HOT SAUCE, TO TASTE

In a bowl, combine ingredients, mixing well. Chill before serving. Serve with any fish or seafood. Yield: 2 cups.

Shrimp and Rice Fritters

1 CUP SHRIMP, PEELED AND DEVEINED
1 EGG
$^1/_4$ CUP WHOLE MILK
1 CUP COOKED RICE
1 CUP FINE CRACKER CRUMBS, DIVIDED
$^1/_4$ CUP ONION, CHOPPED
$^1/_4$ CUP CELERY, CHOPPED
1 TABLESPOON PARSLEY FLAKES
$^3/_4$ TEASPOON CAJUN SEASONING
   OIL FOR FRYING

Grind or chop raw shrimp. Set aside. In a mixing bowl, beat egg and milk. Stir in rice and $^1/_2$ cup cracker crumbs. Add vegetables and seasonings, mixing well. With a tablespoon, scoop heaping spoonfuls and shape into small patties. Dust with remaining cracker crumbs. Fry in one-inch deep hot oil until both sides are golden brown. Drain and serve. Excellent! Yield: 1 dozen depending on size.

Potato Crab Cakes

2	CUPS POTATOES, DICED AND COOKED
1	CUP COOKED OR 2 6-OUNCE CANS CRABMEAT, DRAINED
2	EGGS, BEATEN
$1/2$	CUP SEASONED BREAD CRUMBS, DIVIDED
$1/4$	CUP ONION, CHOPPED
2	TABLESPOONS CANNED PARMESAN CHEESE
2	TABLESPOONS FRESH PARSLEY, CHOPPED
$3/4$	TEASPOON CAJUN SEASONING
	OIL FOR FRYING

In a mixing bowl, mash potatoes with a fork. Stir in crabmeat and eggs. Reserve $1/4$ cup seasoned bread crumbs. Add remaining ingredients, stirring well. With a tablespoon, scoop a heaping spoonful of mixture and shape into cakes. Dust with reserved bread crumbs and fry in one-inch deep hot oil. Fry until golden brown. Drain and serve with Homemade Cocktail Sauce (see p. 5) or tartar sauce. Yield: 5–7 cakes.

Almost any fried appetizer can be changed in size. If a sampling is all you want, make balls. For a larger serving, you'll want a cake or patty. The larger serving can also be served as a main course.

Traditional Crab Cakes

2	EGGS, BEATEN
1	CUP BUTTER CRACKERS, CRUSHED
$1/2$	CUP COOKED OR 6-OUNCE CAN CRABMEAT, DRAINED
1	TABLESPOON FRESH PARSLEY, CHOPPED
$1/2$	TEASPOON CAJUN SEASONING
$1/4$	CUP ONION, CHOPPED
	ALL-PURPOSE FLOUR
	OIL FOR FRYING

In a medium bowl, beat eggs. Stir in cracker crumbs and crabmeat. Add the remaining ingredients. With a tablespoon, scoop spoonfuls and shape into cakes. Dust all sides with flour. Fry in one-inch deep hot oil until both sides are golden brown. Yield: 4–6 crab cakes.

Cajun seasoning is such a convenient and accessible grocery item these days—you can buy it almost anywhere. If you don't have it or prefer not to season with this, a substitute can be made using your own measurements of salt, red pepper, onion powder, and garlic powder. For a homemade version of Cajun seasoning see recipe below.

Cajun Seasoning

13	OUNCES SALT
$1/4$	CUP BLACK PEPPER
$1/2$	CUP RED PEPPER
$1/4$	CUP GARLIC POWDER
$1/4$	CUP ACCENT
$1/4$	CUP ONION POWDER

Combine ingredients. Taste and adjust if necessary. Store in an airtight container. Use in recipes calling for Cajun seasoning. Yield: $2^1/_2$ cups seasoning.

Cheesy Crab Dip

$1/4$	CUP BELL PEPPER, CHOPPED
$1/4$	CUP CELERY, CHOPPED
1	SMALL ONION, CHOPPED
$1/2$	CUP MARGARINE OR BUTTER
$1/2$	CUP ALL-PURPOSE FLOUR
1	12-OUNCE CAN EVAPORATED MILK
$3/4$	POUND COOKED OR 3 6-OUNCE CANS CRABMEAT, DRAINED
1	CUP CHEDDAR CHEESE, GRATED
$1/4$	TEASPOON GARLIC POWDER
$1/4$	TEASPOON RED PEPPER
$1/2$	TEASPOON SALT

Sauté vegetables in margarine or butter. Slowly stir in flour. While stirring, gradually add milk until smooth. Stir in crabmeat, cheese, and seasonings. Heat until cheese melts. Serve warm with chips or crackers, or pour into pastry cups. Yield: 6 cups dip.

Many grocery stores sell crawfish tails in their seafood departments. They're sold in frozen 8- or 16-ounce packages. They are precooked, peeled, and ready to go into recipes. If there is a fishy smell, rinse them before adding to the recipe. If using fresh crawfish, first cook the crawfish (see p. 62 for boiling crawfish), then break off the tails, and peel.

Crawfish Remoulade

Lurline Rodrigue Duplechain is a Lake Charles, Louisiana, native and an excellent Cajun cook. She contributed this crawfish recipe.

$1/4$	CUP CREOLE MUSTARD
$1/2$	CUP VEGETABLE OIL
$1/4$	CUP RED WINE VINEGAR
1	TABLESPOON LEMON JUICE
2	TABLESPOONS WORCESTERSHIRE SAUCE
$1/2$	TEASPOON GARLIC POWDER
1	TABLESPOON KETCHUP
$1/2$	TEASPOON RED HOT SAUCE
1	TEASPOON LEMON ZEST
1	TEASPOON PARSLEY FLAKES
3	TABLESPOONS GREEN ONION, CHOPPED
$1/4$	TEASPOON BLACK PEPPER
1	POUND CRAWFISH TAILS, COOKED AND RINSED
	LETTUCE LEAVES, CHILLED
	CRACKERS

Combine all ingredients in a mixing bowl except crawfish tails. Cover and refrigerate for 24 hours. Stir in freshly rinsed crawfish tails. Serve on chilled lettuce leaves garnished with a pasta salad or a scoop of Seafood and Rice Salad (see p. 75). Serve with crackers. Yield: 16 $1/4$-cup servings.

Crawfish Balls

2	TABLESPOONS FRESH PARSLEY, CHOPPED
$1/4$	CUP GREEN ONION, CHOPPED
2	TABLESPOONS MARGARINE OR BUTTER
2	TABLESPOONS ALL-PURPOSE FLOUR
$1/2$	CUP WHOLE MILK
$1/2$	TEASPOON CAJUN SEASONING
$1/2$	POUND CRAWFISH TAILS, COOKED AND RINSED
2	EGGS, BEATEN
2	CUPS SEASONED BREAD CRUMBS
	OIL FOR FRYING

In a skillet over medium-low heat, sauté vegetables in margarine or butter. Stir in flour. Slowly add milk while whisking continuously over medium-high heat. Cook until mixture boils and becomes thick. Reduce heat and add Cajun seasoning and crawfish. Refrigerate mixture until cooled and ready to handle. With a teaspoon, scoop up spoonfuls and shape into one-inch balls. Dip into the beaten eggs and then in the bread crumbs. Fry in one-inch deep hot oil until all sides are golden brown. Yield: 12–15 balls.

Black-eyed Pea Salsa

Billie Corbin is an Alabama native and a great cook. She contributed this unique recipe.

1	10-OUNCE CAN TOMATOES WITH CHILI PEPPERS, DRAINED
1	15-OUNCE CAN BLACK-EYED PEAS, DRAINED
1	15-OUNCE CAN SHOE PEG CORN, DRAINED
$1/4$	CUP GREEN ONION, CHOPPED
	CHOPPED CILANTRO TO TASTE
	SALT AND PEPPER TO TASTE

Combine all ingredients. Chill for several hours before serving. Serve with chips. Yield: 5 cups salsa.

Favorite Shrimp Mold

2	CUPS SHRIMP, BOILED, PEELED, AND CHOPPED
1	$10^1/_2$-OUNCE CAN CELERY SOUP
1	8-OUNCE PACKAGE CREAM CHEESE
2	$^1/_4$-OUNCE PACKAGES UNFLAVORED GELATIN
$^1/_3$	CUP WATER
$^3/_4$	CUP MAYONNAISE
$^1/_2$	CUP ONION, FINELY CHOPPED
$^3/_4$	CUP CELERY, FINELY CHOPPED
1	TEASPOON CAJUN SEASONING
2	TABLESPOONS WORCESTERSHIRE SAUCE

Prepare shrimp. Set aside. In a saucepan, heat soup and cream cheese until melted. In a small bowl, dissolve gelatin in water. Add to soup mixture. Stir in remaining ingredients. Pour into a greased mold. Refrigerate for several hours or overnight. Invert on a serving platter. Serve with crackers. For a tomato shrimp mold, substitute tomato soup for the celery soup. Yield: 26 $^1/_4$-cup servings.

Mama's Shrimp Dip

My mother, Charlotte Sundberg Saizan, contributed this delicious shrimp dip. A north Florida native, she married and moved to Louisiana as a young adult and quickly added Cajun cooking to her Southern cooking techniques. This dip is always delicious!

2	POUNDS SHRIMP, BOILED, PEELED, AND CHOPPED
1	8-OUNCE PACKAGE CREAM CHEESE, SOFTENED
$^1/_2$	CUP MAYONNAISE
2	TEASPOONS WORCESTERSHIRE SAUCE
1	TEASPOON RED HOT SAUCE
$^1/_4$	CUP GREEN ONION, CHOPPED
3	TABLESPOONS LEMON JUICE

Prepare shrimp; set aside. Combine cream cheese and mayonnaise in mixing bowl. Stir in chopped shrimp along with remaining seasonings, mixing well. Refrigerate for at least 2 hours. Serve with crackers or chips. Yield: 6 cups.

Praline Fruit Dip

This delicious fruit dip was contributed by Jerry and Joyce Rodrigue. It is uniquely different from every other fruit dip I've eaten. Very good!

1	8-OUNCE PACKAGE CREAM CHEESE, SOFTENED
$1/3$	CUP BROWN SUGAR
$1/4$	CUP GRANULATED SUGAR
1	TEASPOON VANILLA
1	6-OUNCE PACKAGE ALMOND BRICKLE CHIPS
2	TABLESPOONS PECANS, CHOPPED

Combine cream cheese and granulated sugar. Let stand for 15 minutes. Stir in remaining ingredients. Chill for several hours. Sprinkle with pecans before serving. Serve with fresh fruit. Yield: $2^1/2$ cups or 10 $1/4$-cup servings.

Pineapple Cheese Ball

2	8-OUNCE PACKAGES CREAM CHEESE, SOFTENED
2	TABLESPOONS ONION, FINELY CHOPPED
$1/4$	CUP GREEN ONION, FINELY CHOPPED
$1/4$	CUP BELL PEPPER, FINELY CHOPPED
1	8-OUNCE CAN PINEAPPLE, DRAINED AND CRUSHED
1	TEASPOON CAJUN SEASONING
1	TEASPOON WORCESTERSHIRE SAUCE
1	CUP PECANS, CHOPPED

Soften cream cheese in medium bowl. Combine remaining ingredients. Mix well. Form into a ball and roll in pecans. Chill overnight before serving. Yield: 20 $1/4$-cup servings.

Cheese and Pecan Wafers

2	CUPS CHEDDAR CHEESE, GRATED
1	CUP ALL-PURPOSE FLOUR
1	CUP PECANS, CHOPPED
1	CUP MARGARINE OR BUTTER, SOFTENED
$1/4$	TEASPOON SALT
$1/4$	TEASPOON RED PEPPER
$1/8$	TEASPOON GARLIC POWDER

Mix all ingredients together. Shape into 2 logs. Wrap in plastic wrap and refrigerate overnight. When ready to bake, preheat oven to 375 degrees. Slice logs into thin wafers. Place on cookie sheet and bake for approximately 8 minutes or until golden brown. Yield: 36 wafers.

Shrimp Puffs

6	TABLESPOONS MARGARINE OR BUTTER
$3/4$	CUP WATER
$3/4$	CUP ALL-PURPOSE FLOUR
$1/4$	TEASPOON GARLIC POWDER
$1/2$	TEASPOON CAJUN SEASONING
3	EGGS
1	CUP SHRIMP, COOKED AND CHOPPED
$1/3$	CUP GREEN ONION, FINELY CHOPPED
$1/3$	CUP PLUS 3 TABLESPOONS PARMESAN CHEESE, GRATED
	ADDITIONAL PARMESAN CHEESE FOR SPRINKLING

Preheat oven to 400 degrees. Place water and margarine or butter in a medium saucepan. Cook over medium heat until margarine or butter has melted. Add flour, garlic powder, and Cajun seasoning. Stir vigorously until dough forms a ball and leaves the sides of the pan. Remove from heat. Let stand 5 minutes. Add eggs one at a time, stirring after each addition. Stir vigorously after the last egg. Stir in shrimp, onion, and $1/3$ cup cheese. Drop rounded teaspoons of dough onto an ungreased cookie sheet, about 2 inches apart. Sprinkle with additional Parmesan cheese. Bake 25–30 minutes or until puffed and golden brown. Serve warm. Yield: 36 puffs.

Crab-Stuffed Banana Peppers

Any pepper can be used. Be sure to use disposable gloves when handling hot peppers.

1	DOZEN SMALL TO MEDIUM BANANA PEPPERS
$^1/_4$	CUP ONION, CHOPPED
$^1/_4$	CUP CELERY, CHOPPED
$^1/_4$	CUP MARGARINE OR BUTTER
1	6-OUNCE CAN CRABMEAT, DRAINED
$^1/_4$	TEASPOON GARLIC POWDER
$^1/_2$	TEASPOON RED HOT SAUCE
1	TEASPOON PARSLEY FLAKES
$^1/_2$	CUP PLAIN BREAD CRUMBS, DIVIDED
2	EGGS, BEATEN, DIVIDED
	WATER
	OIL FOR FRYING

Cut off ends of peppers. Carefully remove seeds from the pepper cavity. Rinse the cavity with water to remove any remaining seeds. Drain and set aside. In a skillet over medium-low heat, sauté vegetables in margarine or butter. Add crabmeat and seasonings. Heat through. Remove from heat and stir in $^1/_4$ cup bread crumbs and one egg. Stuff mixture into the cavities of the peppers. Prepare an egg wash by mixing 3 tablespoons water and one beaten egg. Dip the peppers in the egg wash, then coat with remaining bread crumbs. Fry in a small amount of hot oil until golden brown. Yield: 12 peppers.

Fried Cheese Bites

2	CUPS CHEDDAR CHEESE, GRATED
$^1/_4$	CUP ALL-PURPOSE FLOUR
$^1/_4$	TEASPOON RED PEPPER
4	EGG WHITES, STIFFLY BEATEN
2	CUPS OF VERY FINE CRACKER CRUMBS

In a mixing bowl, combine cheese, flour, and red pepper. Carefully fold in stiffly beaten egg whites. Shape mixture into small balls and roll in cracker crumbs. Drop into hot oil and cook until golden brown. Drain. These are very good! Yield: 24 bites.

Cajun Crackers

1   CUP WHOLE-WHEAT FLOUR
1   CUP ALL-PURPOSE WHITE FLOUR
$1/4$ TEASPOON BAKING SODA
$1/2$ TEASPOON CAJUN SEASONING
$1/2$ TEASPOON GARLIC POWDER
$1/2$ CUP SOUR CREAM
$1/4$ CUP MAYONNAISE
1   TABLESPOON HONEY

Preheat oven to 400 degrees. In a medium bowl, mix together the dry ingredients. With a fork, stir in the mayonnaise, yogurt, and honey. With your hands, divide dough into several balls. On a well-floured surface, using a rolling pin, roll each ball until paper-thin. Sprinkle with additional salt if desired. Bake on an ungreased cookie sheet until lightly browned (approximately 6–8 minutes). After cooling, break into crackers. Store in an airtight container. Yield: 4 dozen, depending on size.

Stuffed Mushrooms

12   LARGE MUSHROOM CAPS
1   6-OUNCE CAN OF CRABMEAT, DRAINED
$1/3$ CUP PLAIN BREAD CRUMBS
4   TABLESPOONS PARMESAN CHEESE, DIVIDED
$1/4$ CUP ONION, FINELY CHOPPED
1   TABLESPOON PARSLEY, CHOPPED
1   EGG, BEATEN
$1/4$ TEASPOON RED PEPPER
$1/4$ CUP MARGARINE OR BUTTER, MELTED

Preheat oven to 350 degrees. Prepare mushrooms by washing, removing, and discarding stems. Set aside. In a bowl, combine all remaining ingredients, reserving 2 tablespoons Parmesan cheese. Mix well. Spoon mixture into the mushroom caps. Drizzle with margarine or butter and sprinkle with reserved Parmesan cheese. Bake for approximately 15 minutes. Yield: 12 appetizers.

Oysters on the Half Shell

24   OYSTERS IN THE SHELL
      LEMON WEDGES
      RED HOT SAUCE, TO TASTE

With a blunt knife, carefully shuck oysters by inserting the knife near the hinge of the oyster. Cut through the muscle that holds the shell together. If desired, drain juice into a bowl to strain for future uses. After draining, place the oyster in the deep half of the shell. Chill if desired. Serve with lemon wedges and hot sauce. Yield: 24 appetizers.

Meatballs Piquant

This is a unique meatball recipe with a delicious sauce. If this recipe appeals to you, you may want to check out the Shrimp Sauce Piquant recipe on page 67.

    1   EGG, BEATEN
    1/4   CUP WHOLE MILK
    3   OUNCES CREAM CHEESE
    1   SMALL ONION, GRATED
    1/4   TEASPOON GARLIC POWDER
    1   TEASPOON PARSLEY
    1   TEASPOON WORCESTERSHIRE SAUCE
    1/2   CUP PLAIN BREAD CRUMBS
    1   POUND GROUND CHUCK
           PIQUANT SAUCE (SEE PAGE 16)

In a medium bowl, beat egg and milk. Soften cream cheese and stir in. Add remaining ingredients except sauce. Mix well. Shape into small 1-inch balls. Cook in a skillet on medium until meatballs are browned. Serve meatballs, with a homemade piquant sauce, from a chafing dish or crock-pot with toothpicks. Yield: 24 meatballs.

Piquant, pronounced **pee caw,** *means "sharp" or "to prick." A piquant sauce is pungent and usually made with vinegar or lemons.*

Piquant Sauce

$^1/_4$ CUP MARGARINE OR BUTTER
1   TABLESPOON WHITE VINEGAR
$1^1/_2$ TEASPOONS KITCHEN BOUQUET FLAVORING
3   TABLESPOONS KETCHUP
1   TEASPOON PREPARED MUSTARD
1   9- OR 10-OUNCE JAR APPLE OR PLUM JELLY

Combine ingredients in a saucepan. Bring to a boil and reduce heat. Heat for several minutes. Serve warm with meatballs.

Holiday Punch

$^1/_2$ GALLON RASPBERRY SHERBET
1   LITER OR 32 OUNCES OF GINGER ALE
$^1/_2$ CAN OR 24-OUNCES PINEAPPLE JUICE
1   .15-OUNCE ENVELOPE UNSWEETENED RASPBERRY DRINK MIX
$^1/_2$ CUP GRANULATED SUGAR

Soften sherbet and place in a punch bowl. Dissolve sugar and drink mix into a small amount of pineapple juice. Pour over sherbet along with remaining liquids. Stir and serve. Strawberry drink mix may be substituted for raspberry.

Spiced Cinnamon Tea

1   28-OUNCE JAR OF ORANGE BREAKFAST DRINK MIX
2   CUPS GRANULATED SUGAR
2   .15-OUNCE PACKAGES UNSWEETENED LEMON DRINK MIX
2   TEASPOONS GROUND CLOVES
2   TEASPOONS GROUND CINNAMON
$^1/_2$ CUP UNSWEETENED INSTANT TEA

Combine dry ingredients and store in an airtight container. Mix 2 heaping teaspoons with a cup of hot water when ready to serve. This recipe can easily be halved. Yield: 25–30 cups of tea.

Spiced Apple Cider

2   QUARTS APPLE CIDER
1   APPLE
    CINNAMON STICKS
1–2 TABLESPOONS WHOLE CLOVES

Pour apple juice in a slow cooker. Core the apple and pierce with the whole cloves. Add to apple juice along with a few cinnamon sticks. Heat for 1 $^1/_2$ to 2 hours on medium or high heat or until steaming hot. Serve with a decorative cinnamon stick if desired. Yield: 2 quarts.

Fruit Tea

My oldest daughter, Cara Corbin Burleson, has worked as a retail manager for several years and loves the fruit tea that a local restaurant serves. She has experimented with many ingredients and has developed an excellent fruit tea.

1   GALLON BREWED TEA, WARM
1   CUP GRANULATED SUGAR
1   12-OUNCE CAN OF ORANGE JUICE, THAWED AND UNDILUTED
1   12-OUNCE CAN OF LEMONADE, THAWED AND UNDILUTED
1   12-OUNCE CAN OF PINEAPPLE JUICE, THAWED AND UNDILUTED
1   LITER GINGER ALE

Dissolve sugar in warm tea. Add remaining ingredients, mixing well. Chill and serve over ice. This recipe can easily be halved. Yield: 25 cups.

Grandma's Lemonade

This lemonade recipe was made frequently by my great grandmother Eva Rodrigue, no doubt for relief from the hot and humid Louisiana weather.

1   CUP LEMON JUICE
1   CUP GRANULATED SUGAR
4   CUPS WATER
    SLICED LEMONS FOR GARNISH

Combine and serve over ice. Yield: 5 cups.

Louisiana is considered the coffee-drinking center of the South. Coffee is the accepted drink at all hours in the home or business. Southern Louisiana prefers strong black coffee in the afternoon, often laced with rum or whiskey. Drinking coffee is a way of communicating and socializing, and refusing to partake when invited for coffee is a breach of etiquette. My cousins Lurline Duplechain and Jerry Rodrigue graciously contributed these coffee recipes.

Nearly Beer Coffee

      STRONG BLACK COFFEE, HOT
2   OUNCES COGNAC
      WHIPPED CREAM, CANNED

Pour strong black coffee into a beer glass. Add cognac and top with 2 inches of whipped cream. This drink looks like a glass of dark beer, hence the name. Serve hot. Yield: single serving.

Choco Coffee

4   CUPS HOT CHOCOLATE MILK
1   CUP VERY STRONG COFFEE, HOT
1   TABLESPOON SHERRY
      PINCH OF SALT
      WHIPPED CREAM, CANNED

Combine all ingredients except whipped cream and serve in individual coffee cups. Top with whipped cream for garnish. Yield 5 cups.

Café Royale

1   CUP BLACK COFFEE, HOT
1   JIGGER BRANDY
      GRANULATED SUGAR TO TASTE

Combine. Serve hot. Yield: single serving.

Café au Lait

3   CUPS STRONG BLACK COFFEE, HOT
3   CUPS LIGHT CREAM

Beat cream until frothy. Fill 6 coffee cups half full of coffee and pour equal parts of cream into the coffee. Serve with a sprinkling of nutmeg or cinnamon. Yield: 6 cups.

Café Rhum

1   CUP STRONG BLACK COFFEE, COOLED
       GRANULATED SUGAR TO TASTE
       ICE CUBES
1   JIGGER RUM
       NUTMEG TO TASTE

Pour sweetened coffee into a glass of ice. Stir in the rum and sprinkle nutmeg on top. Serve chilled.

Coffee Punch

16   CUPS OF COFFEE, COOLED
1   CUP LIGHT CREAM
2   TABLESPOONS GRANULATED SUGAR
1   26-OUNCE BOTTLE COGNAC OR BRANDY
1   GALLON VANILLA ICE CREAM

Prepare coffee. Freeze 6 cups of coffee in a ring mold. Stir in cream, sugar, and cognac to remaining coffee. Pour over ice cream that has been placed in a punch bowl. Float the frozen coffee ring in punch bowl. Serve in punch cups or mugs. Yield: 30 to 35 servings.

Bread & Breakfast

BREAKFAST BREADS AND OTHER DISHES

Calas 22 • Fruit Syrup 22 • Nut Syrup 23 • Banana Nut Bread 23 • Zucchini Nut Bread 24 • Beignets 24 • Black Walnut Bread 25 • Glazed Lemon Nut Bread 26 • Fig Muffins 26 • Fig Bread 27 • Coush Coush 28 • Cheesy Grits Soufflé 29 • Berry Muffins 29 • French Toast 30 • Buttermilk Biscuits 30 • Chocolate Gravy 31 • Strawberry Fig Preserves 31 • Super Easy Fruit Preserves 32

DINNER BREADS

Blue Ribbon Yeast Rolls 33 • Po' Boys 33 • French Bread 34 • Hush Puppies 34 • Spoon Rolls 35 • Sweet Potato Spoon Rolls 35 • Fruit Margarine 36 • Nell's Crunchy Cornbread 36 • Daddy's Sweet Cornbread 36 • Cracklin' Cornbread 37

Center photo: This is a picture of Ralph Prejean at approximately three years of age. The story goes that Ralph was discovered missing by his family one day. Everyone searched frantically for him all through the day. After several hours had passed, he returned home with his wagon and announced he had been "frogging." For an excellent frog leg recipe, see page 88 for Frog Legs Sauce Piquant.

Clockwise from left to right: Lurline Duplechain displays a redfish. My fourth birthday party in Louisiana. Fletcher Corbin with a prized garfish. Gulf Coast shrimp boats. Mardi Gras King cake. Canoes at lake shore. Louisiana crab boil.

21

Calas is a rice cake that was introduced by the African slaves. A New Orleans tradition, these breakfast cakes were once sold by street vendors. They are usually dusted with confectioner's sugar, however they are very good eaten with syrup as you would a pancake.

Calas or Rice Cakes

1	EGG
1	CUP WHOLE MILK
1	TABLESPOON BUTTER, MELTED
1	CUP COOKED RICE
$1^1/_2$	CUPS ALL-PURPOSE FLOUR
$^1/_2$	TEASPOON SALT
2	TABLESPOONS GRANULATED SUGAR
2	TEASPOONS BAKING POWDER

Mix egg, milk, and melted butter. Add rice. Stir in the remaining dry ingredients. Drop by spoonfuls onto a heated, lightly oiled skillet and cook like pancakes. Lightly brown each side. Serve with syrup or sprinkle with confectioner's sugar. Yield: 16–20 cakes.

Fruit Syrup

2	CUPS GRANULATED SUGAR
1	CUP WATER
1	CUP FRUIT, MASHED OR FINELY CHOPPED

Combine all ingredients in a pot. Bring to a boil and cook for 7–8 minutes. Cool and pour into glass or plastic containers. Refrigerate until ready to use. Great on pancakes or rice cakes. Yield: 4 cups.

Nut Syrup

2	CUPS GRANULATED SUGAR
1	CUP WATER
1	CUP BLACK WALNUTS, CHOPPED
2	TEASPOONS BUTTERNUT VANILLA

Combine and boil for 7–8 minutes. Cool and pour in containers. Refrigerate until ready to serve. Yield: 4 cups.

Banana Nut Bread

This banana nut bread recipe comes from my cousin, Lurline Duplechain. She says this is the best banana bread recipe she's ever run across.

$1/2$	CUP SHORTENING
$1^1/2$	CUPS GRANULATED SUGAR
2	EGGS
2	CUPS ALL-PURPOSE FLOUR
$1/2$	TEASPOON BAKING SODA
$1/3$	TEASPOON SALT
$1/4$	CUP BUTTERMILK
$1/2$	TEASPOON VANILLA
1	CUP MASHED BANANAS
$1/2$	CUP PECANS, CHOPPED

Preheat oven to 325 degrees. Cream shortening and sugar. Add eggs, mixing thoroughly. Add sifted dry ingredients alternately with buttermilk and vanilla. Stir in bananas and nuts. Pour into a greased loaf pan and bake for 1 hour. Yield: 8 to 10 servings.

Cajun Cooking Southern Style

Bananas came from the Canary Islands into the New World shortly after its discovery. By the 1800s, bananas had made their way into street markets. The banana plant is a gigantic herb that springs from an underground stem.

Zucchini Nut Bread

1	CUP GRANULATED SUGAR
$1/3$	CUP VEGETABLE OIL
1	EGG
1	CUP ZUCCHINI, SHREDDED
$1^1/2$	CUPS ALL-PURPOSE FLOUR
1	TEASPOON CINNAMON
$1/2$	TEASPOON BAKING SODA
$1/2$	TEASPOON SALT
$1/2$	TEASPOON NUTMEG
$1/4$	TEASPOON BAKING POWDER
$1/2$	CUP WALNUTS, CHOPPED

Preheat oven to 350 degrees. In a mixing bowl, cream together sugar, oil, and egg. Stir in zucchini, mixing well. Stir in dry ingredients. Fold in chopped nuts. Pour into greased and floured loaf pan. Bake for 50–60 minutes. Squash or carrots can be substituted for the zucchini. Yield: 8–10 servings.

Beignets are French doughnuts and another New Orleans tradition. Street vendors popularized this pastry many, many years ago. Be careful not to inhale the confectioner's sugar when you're eating these!

Beignets

1	CUP WHOLE MILK
$1/4$	CUP GRANULATED SUGAR
$1/4$	CUP VEGETABLE OIL
	SALT
$1/2$	TEASPOON NUTMEG
1	$1/4$-OUNCE PACKAGE YEAST
3	CUPS ALL-PURPOSE FLOUR, DIVIDED
1	EGG
	OIL FOR FRYING

In a saucepan, heat milk, sugar, oil, and salt until scalded. Set aside and cool to lukewarm. Meanwhile, combine nutmeg, yeast, and half the flour in a mixing bowl. Add milk and mix with an electric mixer on medium speed for 2 minutes. Add the egg and continue mixing for another 2 minutes. Stir in remaining flour by hand until mixed well. Cover bowl with a towel and refrigerate for 1 hour. Turn dough onto a well-floured surface. Cover again for another 15 minutes. Roll dough into a large rectangle. With a knife or pizza cutter, cut into smaller rectangles approximately 3x2 inches. Cover again for 30 minutes. Fry in hot oil until doughnuts puff or become golden brown. Drain and sprinkle with confectioner's sugar. Yield: approximately 36. Serve warm. To freeze beignets, place in freezer bags after cutting into rectangles. To fry, remove and thaw until room temperature and doubled in size.

Black Walnut Bread

1	CUP GRANULATED SUGAR
$1/4$	CUP SHORTENING
2	EGGS
1	CUP WHOLE MILK
3	CUPS ALL-PURPOSE FLOUR
2	TEASPOONS BAKING POWDER
$1/4$	TEASPOON BAKING SODA
1	TEASPOON SALT
1	TABLESPOON VANILLA
1	CUP BLACK WALNUTS, CHOPPED

Preheat oven to 350 degrees. In a mixing bowl, cream together shortening and sugars. Add eggs. Add dry ingredients alternately with milk. Stir in black walnuts. Pour into 2 greased and floured loaf pans. Bake for 55 minutes. Yield: 16 to 20 servings or 8–10 slices per loaf.

Cajun Cooking Southern Style

Black walnut trees mature at 150 years old and can live to be as old as 250 years. Found in eastern North America, the tree is also cultivated for a dye found in the fruit husk.

Glazed Lemon Nut Bread

This delicious bread recipe was contributed by Joyce Rodrigue, a Lake Charles, Louisiana, native.

$1/4$	CUP MARGARINE OR BUTTER, SOFTENED
$3/4$	CUP GRANULATED SUGAR
2	EGGS
2	CUPS ALL-PURPOSE FLOUR
$2^1/2$	TEASPOONS BAKING POWDER
1	TEASPOON SALT
$3/4$	CUP WHOLE MILK
2	TEASPOONS LEMON ZEST
$1/2$	CUP NUTS, CHOPPED
$1/4$	CUP CONFECTIONER'S SUGAR
1	TEASPOON LEMON JUICE

Preheat oven to 350 degrees. In a mixing bowl, cream together margarine or butter and granulated sugar. Add eggs, beat well. Add dry ingredients to mixture along with milk. Stir in lemon zest and nuts. Pour batter in greased loaf pan and bake for 45–50 minutes. Meanwhile, combine confectioner's sugar and lemon juice for glaze. Spread on hot loaf. Yield 8 to 10 servings.

Fig Muffins

1	CUP GRANULATED SUGAR
$1/2$	CUP SHORTENING
2	EGGS
$1/2$	CUP WHOLE MILK
2	CUPS ALL-PURPOSE FLOUR
1	TEASPOON SALT
1	CUP FIGS, DRIED AND COARSELY CHOPPED
$1/2$	CUP NUTS, CHOPPED

Preheat oven to 400 degrees. In a mixing bowl, cream together sugar and shortening. Add eggs. Mix well. Mix dry ingredients alternately with milk. Fold in figs and nuts. Fill greased muffin pans $3/4$ full. Bake for 20 minutes. Yield: 15 muffins.

Figs were once called the poor man's food. A native to the Mediterranean, the fruit was introduced to Louisiana in the 1700s by the influx of Europeans. The fruit and tree were once held as sacred and are mentioned often in the Bible. If you like these fig recipes, you'll like fig cake on page 119.

Fig Bread

1	CUP SHORTENING
1	CUP GRANULATED SUGAR
1	CUP BROWN SUGAR
3	EGGS
$2^1/_2$	CUPS ALL-PURPOSE FLOUR
3	TEASPOONS BAKING POWDER
$1/_4$	TEASPOON SALT
1	TEASPOON NUTMEG
$1/_2$	TEASPOON CLOVES
$1/_2$	TEASPOON ALLSPICE
$1/_2$	CUP WHOLE MILK
1	CUP DRIED FIGS, CHOPPED
$1/_2$	CUP RAISINS
$1/_2$	CUP NUTS, CHOPPED

Preheat oven to 325 degrees. In a mixing bowl, cream together shortening and sugars. Add eggs. Stir well. Add dry ingredients alternately with milk. Fold in figs, raisins, and nuts. Pour into 2 greased and floured loaf pans. Bake for 1 hour. Yield: 16 to 20 servings.

Coush Coush, pronounced cushcush, is a cornmeal mush, fried brown and eaten with milk and sugar poured over, usually at breakfast. Originally known as couscous in the Far East, the slaves brought this cornmeal dish to Louisiana from the West Indies. According to my Aunt Doris, my great-great grandparents fixed it often and served it with fresh or preserved figs. My father's favorite version was to simply eat leftover cornbread crumbled up with milk and sugar for dessert after supper.

Coush Coush

Lurline Duplechain contributed this coush coush recipe.

$1/2$ CUP OIL
2   CUPS CORNMEAL
$3/4$ CUP WHOLE MILK
$3/4$ CUP WATER
1   TEASPOON BAKING POWDER
1   TEASPOON SALT

Heat oil in a skillet. Meanwhile, mix remaining ingredients. Pour batter into medium hot oil. Let crust form on bottom before stirring. Reduce heat to low, and cook an additional 15 minutes, stirring occasionally to keep batter from sticking or breaking up. Cook till slightly brown. Serve as you would cereal, with milk and sugar on top. Yield: 8 $1/2$-cup servings.

Cheesy Grits Soufflé

1	CUP GRITS
3	CUPS WATER
2	EGGS, BEATEN
1	8-OUNCE JAR JALAPENO CHEESE SPREAD
$1/4$	CUP MARGARINE OR BUTTER
1	CUP CHEDDAR CHEESE, GRATED AND DIVIDED

Preheat oven to 350 degrees. In a heavy saucepan, combine grits and water and cook until it thickens and the water is absorbed. While warm, stir in the eggs, cheese spread, margarine or butter, and half the cheese. Pour into a casserole dish and top with remaining grated cheese. Bake 45–50 minutes or until set. Yield: 8 servings.

A true southern staple, grits are made from coarsely ground dried hominy. Cheesy grits soufflé is a new twist on an old favorite.

Berry Muffins

$1/4$	CUP SHORTENING
$1/3$	CUP GRANULATED SUGAR
2	EGGS
$1/2$	TEASPOON VANILLA
2	CUPS ALL-PURPOSE FLOUR
4	TEASPOONS BAKING POWDER
$3/4$	TEASPOON SALT
$2/3$	CUP WHOLE MILK
$2/3$	CUP BERRIES

Preheat oven to 400 degrees. In a mixing bowl, cream together shortening and sugar. Add eggs and vanilla, mixing well. Sift dry ingredients reserving $1/3$ cup to dust berries with. Stir in dry ingredients, alternating with milk. Gradually fold in berries and remaining flour. Bake in greased muffin pans for approximately 25–30 minutes. Blackberries and blueberries are excellent in this recipe. Yield: 12 muffins.

French Toast or *Pain Perdu*

$1/2$ CUP WHOLE MILK

1   EGG, BEATEN

1   TABLESPOON GRANULATED SUGAR AND $1/4$ TEASPOON
      CINNAMON, MIXED

$1/2$ TEASPOON VANILLA

      DASH OF SALT

4–5   SLICES OF STALE FRENCH BREAD

In a mixing bowl, combine egg, milk, cinnamon sugar, vanilla, and salt. Dip bread slices in mixture, coating both sides. In a skillet over low heat, lightly brown both sides of bread in butter or vegetable oil. Sprinkle with cinnamon sugar, confectioner's sugar, syrup, or honey. Yield: 4–5 servings.

Pain Perdu **is French for "lost bread." This version of French toast was made with old or stale French bread that would normally be thrown out or "lost."**

Buttermilk Biscuits

1    $1/4$-OUNCE PACKAGE YEAST

$1/2$ CUP WARM WATER

1   CUP BUTTERMILK

$1/4$ CUP SHORTENING

$3/4$ TEASPOON SALT

1   TEASPOON BAKING POWDER

3–3$1/2$ CUPS ALL-PURPOSE FLOUR

Preheat oven to 400 degrees. In a small bowl, mix yeast and warm water. Set aside. On the stovetop, heat buttermilk and shortening to scalding in a medium-sized saucepan. Remove from heat and cool to lukewarm. Stir in the yeast and the dry ingredients, beginning with 3 of the 3 $1/2$ cups of flour. Add all or part of the remaining flour if necessary to make stiff dough. Turn onto a floured surface and knead until the dough is firm and elastic-like. With a rolling pin, roll the dough to a $1/2$-inch thickness. Cut out with a biscuit cutter. Place biscuits on a baking pan and cover. Let rise for 1 hour. Bake at 400 degrees for 15 minutes. Serve with Chocolate Gravy. Yield: 24 biscuits.

Chocolate Gravy

This recipe is contributed by my daughter, Aimee Corbin. This was one of her favorite recipes from her home economics class at school. It is delicious and unique!

$1/4$	CUP COCOA
$1/4$	CUP ALL-PURPOSE FLOUR
1	CUP GRANULATED SUGAR
$2^1/_2$	CUPS WHOLE MILK
3	TABLESPOONS MARGARINE OR BUTTER
$1^1/_2$	TEASPOONS VANILLA
	DASH OF SALT

Heat milk in a saucepan or microwaveable container until it begins to boil. In another saucepan, combine dry ingredients. Add about 1 cup of the warm milk, stirring slowly. After ingredients are well combined, add remaining milk, stirring until the mixture has thickened. Stir in remaining ingredients. Serve with buttermilk biscuits. Yield: 3 cups.

Strawberry Fig Preserves

My mother came across this recipe about 30 years ago. It is incredibly easy and absolutely the best preserves you'll ever taste. By simply altering the fruit and gelatin flavor, the flavor possibilities are endless!

3	CUPS FIGS, MASHED AND PEELED
3	CUPS GRANULATED SUGAR
1	6-OUNCE PACKAGE STRAWBERRY GELATIN

Combine in saucepan and cook over medium heat, stirring occasionally until thickened, approximately 15 minutes. Pour into small glass jars and seal tightly. Refrigerate. Serve with biscuits. Yield: 3 cups.

Super Easy Fruit Preserves

3   CUPS FRESH FRUIT

3   CUPS GRANULATED SUGAR

1   6 OZ. PACKAGE FRUIT FLAVORED GELATIN

Wash fruit. Chop and mash larger fruits. In a medium saucepan, combine fruit with sugar and similar flavored gelatin. Cook over medium heat, stirring occasionally for approximately 15 minutes or until thickened. Pour into small glass jars, and seal tightly. Refrigerate. Yield: 3 cups.

BREAD MAKING TECHNIQUES

- When a recipe gives a range for the flour amount, start by adding the minimal amount and add as much of the remaining flour as you can.
- Kneading dough develops the gluten of the flour, which determines the overall texture when finished. To knead, place dough on a well-floured surface, place the heel of your hand into the dough, and push away. Make a quarter turn with the dough and fold over. Repeat process continually until the dough has a smooth and elastic appearance.
- The best temperature for dough rising is 80–85 degrees. Temperatures that are too hot can kill the yeast. Cold temperatures can stunt the yeast's growth. Dough should rise until doubled in size.
- It is important to check the freshness date on the package of yeast for successful baking. Yeast keeps best in a cool dry place such as a pantry, away from the stove or oven.
- Breads rise more quickly in higher altitudes.
- When a recipe calls for the dough to be covered, it is important to use a porous cloth because the yeast is alive and needs to breathe to continue growing.
- When baking breads, as with all other baked items, it is important to have the oven preheated because the baking time specified is always with a preheated oven—not a cold oven.

Blue Ribbon Yeast Rolls

$5^1/_2$–$6^1/_2$	CUPS ALL-PURPOSE FLOUR
$^1/_2$	CUP GRANULATED SUGAR
$1^1/_2$	TEASPOON SALT
2	$^1/_4$-OUNCE PACKAGES YEAST
$1^1/_4$	CUPS WARM WATER
$^1/_2$	CUP WHOLE MILK
$^1/_3$	CUP MARGARINE OR BUTTER, MELTED
2	EGGS

Preheat oven to 400 degrees. In a large mixing bowl, combine 2 cups of flour with sugar, salt, and dry yeast. Set aside. In a saucepan, combine water and milk. Heat to warm but not hot. Pour over flour mixture. Add margarine or butter and eggs, stirring well. Add another 2 cups of flour and beat with a mixer for 2 minutes. Stir in by hand as much of the remaining flour is needed to form a stiff dough. Turn onto a well-floured surface and knead for 10 minutes. Return to bowl and cover with a cloth. Let rise for one hour or until dough has doubled. Punch dough and divide into 2 sections. Place on a floured surface and roll sections into circles about ¼-inch thick and 12 inches or so in diameter. Cut circles into pizza-shaped triangles. Roll up crescent style and place on a greased baking sheet. Let rise another hour or until doubled. Bake at 400 degrees for 12–15 minutes. Yield: 24 crescent rolls.

The story goes that the Po' Boy sandwich got its name from the New Orleans streetcar strike. The street vendors made the sandwich especially for the strikers and sold it to them at an economical price. Upon seeing a striker, the vendor would announce "another po boy."

Po' Boys

Follow directions for French Bread (see p. 34). Divide each dough half into thirds. Shape each third into a cylinder shape or a mini French bread, so that you have 6 mini-loaves. Place on a greased baking sheet and cover with a towel. Let them rise until doubled or for about 30 minutes. Bake at 450 degrees for 25 minutes. After cooling, cut each mini-loaf in half lengthwise and fill with fried seafood. See page 64 for Fried Shrimp. Yield 6 mini-loaves.

French Bread

$2^1/_2$	CUPS WARM WATER
2	$^1/_4$-OUNCE PACKAGES YEAST
1	TABLESPOON SALT
1	TABLESPOON GRANULATED SUGAR
1	TABLESPOON SHORTENING, MELTED
6–6$^1/_2$	CUPS ALL-PURPOSE FLOUR, SIFTED
	SESAME SEEDS, OPTIONAL

In a small bowl, dissolve yeast in warm water. Add salt, sugar, shortening, and flour, stirring well. Cover bowl and place in a warm corner. Let dough rise until doubled, approximately 1 hour. Divide dough in half and turn onto well-floured board. Roll each section into a large rectangle. Roll dough onto itself, beginning with the wide side. Pinch the sides together to seal. Sprinkle rolls with sesame seeds if desired. Place on a greased cookie sheet and cover. Let rise again until doubled, about 1 hour. Cut several diagonal slashes on top of loaves with a sharp knife. Preheat oven to 450 degrees. Bake for 25 minutes. Yield: 2 loaves.

The story goes that the hush puppy got its name when fried cornbread droppings were made from leftover batter and fed to yapping dogs to hush them up. Here's my favorite recipe!

Hush Puppies

2	CUPS YELLOW CORNMEAL
$^1/_4$	CUP ALL-PURPOSE FLOUR
1	TEASPOON BAKING SODA
1	TEASPOON BAKING POWDER
$^1/_8$	TEASPOON GARLIC POWDER
$1^1/_2$	TEASPOONS SALT
1	CUP WHOLE MILK
1	EGG
2	TABLESPOONS ONION, FINELY CHOPPED
	OIL FOR FRYING

Mix dry ingredients in a bowl. Add milk, egg, and onion. Stir well. Drop by tablespoonfuls into hot cooking oil. Fry until golden brown. Yield: 30–35 servings.

Spoon Rolls

Doris Rodrigue Hancock is the eldest of the Rodrigue family at 82 years young. She was born the youngest in a family of ten kids. Having had eight children of her own, she has certainly done her share of cooking and keeping kids happy. Spoon Rolls is one of her recipe contributions.

2	CUPS WARM WATER
1/4	CUP GRANULATED SUGAR
1	1/4-OUNCE PACKAGE YEAST
1/2	CUP VEGETABLE OIL
1	EGG, BEATEN
4	CUPS SELF-RISING FLOUR
1/4	TEASPOON SALT

In a large mixing bowl, mix ingredients in the order listed. Cover and refrigerate for one hour. Preheat oven to 450 degrees. Spoon dough into greased muffin tins and bake for 13 to 15 minutes or until golden brown. Yield: 24 rolls.

Sweet Potato Spoon Rolls

4	CUPS ALL-PURPOSE FLOUR
1/4	CUP GRANULATED SUGAR
1	TEASPOON SALT
1	1/4-OUNCE PACKAGE YEAST
1	CUP WHOLE MILK
1/4	CUP MARGARINE OR BUTTER
1	EGG
1	16-OUNCE CAN SWEET POTATOES, MASHED

In a mixing bowl, combine 1 cup of flour with sugar, salt, and yeast. In a skillet, heat milk and margarine or butter to scalding. Cool to lukewarm and pour over dry mixture. Add the egg and sweet potatoes, and mix with an electric mixer on medium speed until well combined. Stir in the remaining 3 cups of flour by hand. Cover and let rise 1 hour or until doubled. Punch the air out of the dough and spoon tablespoonfuls into greased muffin tins. Cover and let rise for another 30 minutes. Preheat oven to 375 degrees. Bake 13–15 minutes. Yield: approximately 24 rolls.

Fruit Margarine

$1/2$ CUP MARGARINE OR BUTTER, SOFTENED
$1/4$ CUP FRUIT PRESERVES
        DASH OF SALT

In a bowl, combine all ingredients and chill before serving. Serve with your favorite bread. Yield: $3/4$ cup fruit margarine.

Nell's Crunchy Cornbread

1   CUP SELF-RISING CORNMEAL
$1/8$ CUP VEGETABLE OIL
$3/4$ CUP WHOLE MILK

Preheat oven to 400 degrees. In a mixing bowl, mix together all ingredients. Pour batter into a cake pan that has been sprayed or coated with vegetable oil. Bake for 40 minutes. Yield: 8 slices.

Daddy's Sweet Cornbread

$1^1/2$ CUPS YELLOW CORNMEAL
$1/2$ CUP ALL-PURPOSE FLOUR
$1/3$ CUP GRANULATED SUGAR
$1/2$ TEASPOON SALT
$1/2$ TEASPOON BAKING SODA
$1/2$ TEASPOON BAKING POWDER
$1/4$ CUP VEGETABLE OIL
1   EGG
$1^1/2$ CUPS BUTTERMILK

Preheat oven to 375 degrees. Combine dry ingredients in a mixing bowl. Stir in vegetable oil, egg, and buttermilk, mixing well. Bake in a greased loaf pan for 55–60 minutes. Yield: 8–10 slices.

Cracklin' Cornbread

Lurline Rodrigue Duplechain contributed this Cracklin' Cornbread recipe.

3	TABLESPOONS VEGETABLE OIL
$1^1/_2$	CUPS YELLOW CORNMEAL
$^1/_2$	CUP ALL-PURPOSE FLOUR
$^1/_2$	TEASPOON BAKING POWDER
$^1/_2$	TEASPOON SALT
2	TABLESPOONS GRANULATED SUGAR
1	EGG
$^3/_4$	CUP WHOLE MILK
$1^1/_2$	CUPS CRACKLINS

Preheat oven to 375 degrees. In a heavy 10-inch skillet, heat oil until hot. Meanwhile, combine ingredients in a mixing bowl. Pour batter into hot skillet. Place skillet in oven and bake for approximately 40 minutes or until golden and crusty. Yield: 8–10 slices.

My great-grandparents raised hogs for a living. Making cracklins out of pig fat was one more way of making use of the pig. The story goes, according to my mother, that all of the pig was used except the squeal.

Vegetables, Rice, & Roux

Center photo: Shirley Micelli displays a vegetable casserole at the family reunion.

Clockwise from left to right: Louisiana crab boil. Lurline Duplechain prepares a roux in her kitchen. Caleb and John Corbin. Fletcher Corbin. Jon Prejean and daughter Chantelle with their catch. Mardi Gras King cake. Ralph Prejean.

Maque Choux or Fried Corn

10	EARS OF FRESH CORN OR
	1 32-OUNCE BAG FROZEN KERNEL CORN
5–6	STRIPS OF BACON
$1/2$	CUP ONION, CHOPPED
$1/2$	CUP BELL PEPPER, CHOPPED
1	GARLIC CLOVE
	SALT AND PEPPER TO TASTE

Shuck corn. Scrape kernels into a bowl. Set aside. In a large skillet, cook bacon and other vegetables until bacon is somewhat crunchy and vegetables are tender. Stir in corn and simmer for approximately 25–30 minutes. Add a sprinkling of sugar if desired. Yield: 8–10 servings.

Maque choux (pronounced **mock shoo**) *is an Indian dish consisting of fried corn and vegetables. This dish has been part of the Louisiana culture for a very long time. This is the basic fried corn recipe, however almost any vegetable can be added to the corn if desired, including creamed corn for a creamier dish.*

Corn Fritters

1	15-OUNCE CAN WHOLE KERNEL CORN, DRAINED
1	TEASPOON SALT
	PEPPER TO TASTE
$1/2$	CUP ALL-PURPOSE FLOUR
2	EGGS
1	TABLESPOON ONION, MINCED
1	TABLESPOON BELL PEPPER, MINCED
	OIL FOR FRYING

Combine ingredients, mixing well. Drop by tablespoonfuls into $1/4$-inch deep hot oil. Pan fry both sides until golden brown. Yield: 15–18 fritters.

Corn and Tomato Pie

1$^1/_2$	CUPS PLAIN BREAD CRUMBS, DIVIDED IN THIRDS
2	LARGE TOMATOES, PEELED AND SLICED, DIVIDED
$^1/_2$	CUP BELL PEPPER, CHOPPED, DIVIDED
1	TEASPOON SALT, DIVIDED
1	TEASPOON GRANULATED SUGAR, DIVIDED
$^1/_4$	TEASPOON PEPPER, DIVIDED
3	CUPS CORN, FROZEN, DIVIDED

Preheat oven to 375 degrees. In a casserole dish, layer a third of the bread crumbs. Over that, layer half of each ingredient in the order it is listed. Add another third of the bread crumbs. Layer remaining ingredients on top and finally the last of the bread crumbs. Sprinkle with melted margarine or butter if desired. Bake for 35 minutes. Yield: 6–8 servings.

Corn Pudding

This delicious corn pudding was contributed by my sister Laurie Saizan Hood. Laurie is a Sulphur, Louisiana, native and a full-time working mom of four girls. With very little time to spare, Laurie has created this simple and great tasting corn pudding. This dish is a great accompaniment to ham or turkey.

3	15-OUNCE CANS CREAMED CORN
3	15-OUNCE CANS WHOLE KERNEL CORN, DRAINED
3	EGGS
1	CUP GRANULATED SUGAR
1	CUP ALL-PURPOSE FLOUR
$^1/_2$	CUP MARGARINE OR BUTTER, SOFTENED
$^1/_2$	TEASPOON SALT

Preheat oven to 400 degrees. Combine all ingredients. Pour into a greased casserole dish. Bake for 30 minutes or until golden and set. Yield: 12–14 servings.

Eggplant Casserole

2	MEDIUM EGGPLANTS, PEELED AND CUBED
1	CUP ONION, CHOPPED
1	CUP BELL PEPPER, CHOPPED
1	GARLIC CLOVE, MINCED
3	EGGS, BEATEN
1	TABLESPOON WORCESTERSHIRE SAUCE
1	10-OUNCE CAN TOMATOES WITH CHILI PEPPERS
1	$10^1/_2$-OUNCE CAN CREAM OF MUSHROOM SOUP
$^1/_4$	CUP MARGARINE OR BUTTER, SOFTENED
2	CUPS CHEDDAR CHEESE, GRATED AND DIVIDED
1	CUP CRACKER CRUMBS

Preheat oven to 350 degrees. Boil eggplant and onion in salted water. Drain. Add remaining ingredients except half of cheese and the cracker crumbs. Pour eggplant mixture into a casserole dish. Top with crumbs and bake for 20 minutes. Remove from oven and sprinkle remaining cheese on top. Bake an additional 10–15 minutes or until cheese is melted. Yield: 8–10 servings.

Squash Fritters

2	CUPS FRESH SUMMER SQUASH, CHOPPED OR SHREDDED
1	EGG, BEATEN
1	CUP ALL-PURPOSE FLOUR
2	TABLESPOONS GRANULATED SUGAR
2	TEASPOONS BAKING POWDER
$^1/_2$	TEASPOON SALT

Combine shredded squash and beaten egg in a large bowl. Add remaining ingredients, mixing well. Drop by tablespoonfuls into a small amount of hot vegetable oil in a frying pan. Pan fry both sides in $^1/_4$-inch deep oil until golden brown. Drain fritters and sprinkle with confectioner's sugar. Serve warm. Yield: 12–14 fritters.

Favorite Spinach Casserole

1   10-OUNCE FROZEN SPINACH, CHOPPED
1   $10^{1}/_{2}$-OUNCE CAN CREAM OF MUSHROOM SOUP
1   3-OUNCE PACKAGE CREAM CHEESE, SOFTENED
1   2.8-OUNCE CAN FRIED ONION RINGS

Preheat oven to 350 degrees. Cook and drain spinach thoroughly. Stir in soup, softened cream cheese, and half the can of onion rings. Pour into a casserole dish and top with remaining onion rings. Bake for approximately 30 minutes or until bubbly. Yield: 6–8 servings.

Favorite Squash Casserole

1   POUND SUMMER SQUASH, PEELED AND CUBED
$1/_{2}$ CUP ONION, CHOPPED
1   EGG, BEATEN
$1/_{4}$ CUP MARGARINE OR BUTTER, SOFTENED
$1/_{2}$ TEASPOON SALT
1   TABLESPOON GRANULATED SUGAR
$1/_{4}$ TEASPOON PAPRIKA
$1/_{2}$ CUP BUTTER CRACKER CRUMBS
1   CUP CHEESE, GRATED AND DIVIDED

Boil squash and onion in salted water until tender. Drain and mash. Preheat oven to 350 degrees. Pour squash mixture into a casserole dish and add the egg, margarine or butter, salt, sugar, paprika, and half of the cheese. Sprinkle with cracker crumbs and bake for approximately 20 minutes. Sprinkle remaining cheese on top and bake an additional 10 minutes or until cheese melts. Yield: 6–8 servings.

Creole Tomato Casserole

5	LARGE TOMATOES
2	CUPS SEASONED BREAD CRUMBS
$1/_3$	CUP PARMESAN CHEESE
1	TABLESPOON ONION, MINCED
$1/_4$	TEASPOON GARLIC POWDER
$1/_2$	TEASPOON SALT
1	TEASPOON RED HOT SAUCE
1	TEASPOON GRANULATED SUGAR
1	CUP CHEESE, GRATED

Preheat oven to 350 degrees. Cut out tomato stems. Chop tomatoes and mix with remaining ingredients. Pour into a casserole dish and top with grated cheese. Bake for approximately 30 minutes. Yield: 6–8 servings.

Grandpa's White Beans and Bacon

Grandpa's White Beans and Bacon was a dish often cooked by my grandfather Jim Saizan Sr. My cousin Dr. Jacque de la Bretonne remembers eating this dish as a young boy while his uncle Jimmy babysat him. My mother, Charlotte Saizan, contributed this recipe.

1	POUND WHITE NORTHERN OR NAVY BEANS
$1/_2$	POUND BACON
1	CUP ONION, CHOPPED
2	GARLIC CLOVES, CHOPPED
1	TABLESPOON SALT
	BLACK AND RED PEPPER TO TASTE
	RICE, COOKED (SEE PP. 49–50)

Rinse beans. Cover with water and soak overnight. The next day, bring to a boil and simmer for 1 hour. Add half the bacon, and all of the vegetables, salt, and pepper. Continue cooking over low heat for another hour or until beans are tender. Meanwhile, cook and drain remaining bacon. Crumble and sprinkle over beans. Serve over hot rice with cornbread (see p. 36–37). Yield: 6–8 servings.

Both red beans and rice and white beans and bacon are economical and truly southern classics.

Red Beans and Rice

1	POUND DRIED RED BEANS
1	HAM HOCK
1$^1/_2$	CUPS ONION, CHOPPED
2	GARLIC CLOVES, CHOPPED
$^1/_2$	TEASPOON RED PEPPER
1	TEASPOON SALT
1	TABLESPOON SMOKE-FLAVORED LIQUID SEASONING
1	POUND SMOKED SAUSAGE, SLICED
	RICE, COOKED (SEE PP. 49–50)

Rinse red beans. Cover with water and soak overnight. The next day, add ham hock and remaining ingredients except sausage. Cover and cook over low heat until the beans are tender, about 2 hours or so. Add more water if necessary to keep the beans from sticking. Add sliced sausage the last 15 minutes or so and cook uncovered for 15 minutes. Serve over hot rice. Yield: 8–10 servings.

Praline Sweet Potatoes

Sweet potatoes and yams are abundant Louisiana crops often used interchangeably in many dishes. This is my favorite sweet potato casserole! The butternut flavoring adds a special taste to this dish.

1	29-OUNCE CAN SWEET POTATOES, DRAINED
$1/4$	CUP MARGARINE OR BUTTER
$1/2$	CUP EVAPORATED MILK
1	CUP GRANULATED SUGAR
2	EGGS
$1/4$	TEASPOON SALT
$1/2$	TEASPOON VANILLA
$1/2$	TEASPOON BUTTERNUT FLAVORING

Mix all ingredients with a mixer until well blended. Pour mixture into a casserole dish and sprinkle with prepared topping.

TOPPING:

$1/2$	CUP BROWN SUGAR
$1/2$	CUP PECANS, CHOPPED
$1/4$	CUP MARGARINE OR BUTTER
$1/2$	CUP ALL-PURPOSE FLOUR

Preheat oven to 350 degrees. Cut margarine or butter into pieces. Cut remaining ingredients into margarine or butter with a pastry blender. Sprinkle over casserole. Bake for 30 minutes. Yield: 8–10 servings.

Creamy Potato Salad

6	MEDIUM NEW OR RED POTATOES
$1/2$	CUP CELERY, FINELY CHOPPED
$1/4$	CUP GREEN ONION, FINELY CHOPPED
1	TABLESPOON SWEET PICKLE RELISH
$1/2$	CUP MAYONNAISE
$1/2$	CUP SOUR CREAM
	SALT AND PEPPER TO TASTE

Wash and cube potatoes. Boil potatoes until tender, approximately 20 minutes. Drain and stir in remaining ingredients. Serve warm or chilled. Yield: 8–10 servings.

Country Cole Slaw

This unique cole slaw recipe has been contributed by Mildred Corbin Barton. Mildred is an Alabama native and an excellent southern cook.

4	CUPS SHREDDED CABBAGE
1	12-OUNCE CAN CORN WITH SWEET PEPPERS, DRAINED
$1/2$	CUP ONION, FINELY CHOPPED
$1/4$	CUP CHEDDAR CHEESE, SHREDDED

In a large bowl, combine ingredients and mix with Creamy Mustard Dressing. Chill and serve. Yield: 8–10 servings.

Creamy Mustard Dressing

1	CUP MAYONNAISE
2	TABLESPOONS VINEGAR
1	TEASPOON MUSTARD, PREPARED
$1/2$	TEASPOON CELERY SEED

Combine and pour over Country Cole Slaw.

Old-Fashioned Macaroni and Cheese

The oldest living relative representing the Rodrigue family is Mable Deslatte Robicheaux. She is a Louisiana native and is ninety-plus years young. Oh, the stories she could tell! She contributed this Old Fashioned Macaroni and Cheese. It is delicious!

1	CUP ELBOW MACARONI, UNCOOKED
$1^1/_2$	CUPS CHEDDAR CHEESE, GRATED
3	EGGS, BEATEN
$1^1/_3$	CUPS EVAPORATED MILK
	SALT TO TASTE

In a large pot, cook macaroni according to directions. Drain. Return to saucepan. Add remaining ingredients and cook over low heat until thick, approximately 30 minutes. Serve warm. Yield: 6–8 servings.

Stewed Okra and Tomatoes

1	POUND FRESH OKRA
$1/_4$	CUP ONION, CHOPPED
2	MEDIUM TOMATOES
	VEGETABLE OIL
	SALT AND PEPPER TO TASTE

Rinse okra and tomatoes. Okra may be whole or cut into slices. Quarter tomatoes. Place okra, onion, and tomatoes in a skillet that has been coated or sprayed with vegetable oil. Add salt and pepper. Cover and cook on medium-low heat for 40 to 45 minutes or until okra is tender. Frozen okra may be used, as well as canned tomatoes. Yield: 4–6 servings.

Vegetable Batter

1	CUP ALL-PURPOSE FLOUR
1	CUP WHOLE MILK
1	EGG, BEATEN
$1/4$	CUP VEGETABLE OIL
1	TEASPOON BAKING SODA
	VEGETABLE OIL FOR FRYING

Mix all ingredients except for the frying oil. Dip sliced vegetables into the batter and drop into hot oil. Fry until golden. Squash, zucchini, mushrooms, and onion rings are excellent in this batter. Yield: $2^1/_2$ cups.

No-Measuring Rice

My Dad taught me this very simple way of cooking rice.

Fill a small pot half full of white long grain rice. Rinse rice 2 to 3 times or until water is no longer cloudy. To measure the appropriate water amount, pour a small amount of water over rice (1 to 2 inches). Place your index finger into the water. Do not penetrate the rice. The water should reach the first finger joint (not the knuckle). This method is virtually foolproof, however it is not recommended for large rice portions. Add approximately 1 teaspoon of salt for every cup of rice. Bring rice to a boil and reduce heat to low. Stir, cover pot, and cook for approximately 25 minutes. Perfect!

Stove Top Rice

2	PARTS WATER
1	PART WHITE LONG GRAIN RICE
1	TEASPOON SALT PER CUP OF RICE

Rinse rice if desired. Place in a large pot. Add water and salt. Bring rice to a boil and reduce heat to low. Stir, cover pot, and cook for approximately 25 minutes. Yield: 1 cup uncooked equals 2 cups cooked; 2 cups uncooked equals 4 cups cooked.

Microwave Rice

In a glass bowl, combine 2 parts water to 1 part white long grain rice. For every cup of rice, add 1 teaspoon salt. For small portions, microwave covered on high for 10 minutes. Let stand for an additional 10 minutes. For larger portions, increase cooking time by 5 minutes for every half-cup of rice. Rotate dish every 5 minutes while cooking.

SMALL PORTION

2 CUPS WATER
1 CUP RICE
1 TEASPOON SALT

LARGE PORTION

3 CUPS WATER
$1^1/_2$ CUPS RICE
$1^1/_2$ TEASPOONS SALT

Reheated Rice

Leftover rice can reheat well on the stove top over low heat. Add about a tablespoon of water for every half cup of cooked rice. Heat for 20 minutes or so. Rice will be good as new! A quicker method can be done in the microwave. Transfer rice into a zippered bag or covered microwave container. Heat on a medium setting until rice begins to steam. Time will depend on the amount being heated.

ROUX

In the beginning there was roux . . . and it was very, very good. *Well, roux by itself isn't that tasty, but it is one of the most important ingredients in Cajun cooking. Roux is French for reddish brown or russet. Roux not only adds an interesting flavor to many soups and stews, but also is a thickener in some dishes as well. I modify standard roux recipes by using 2 parts flour to 1 part vegetable oil. This is less greasy than most roux and lower in fat. I have included several roux recipes in this section: one is fat free, but a little time consuming. Roux is not particularly hard to make, but it requires continuous attention and stirring to make sure the roux doesn't burn. Roux resembles a paste at first, then becomes thinner as the starch breaks down. When you're close to your desired color (medium to dark brown is what I aim for), add onions or any other chopped vegetables you like. Continue cooking roux for 10 to 15 minutes, until the vegetables become soft. Continue to stir so it will not burn. The entire roux process takes about 50 to 60 minutes. My father would often double the roux and freeze half for another day. Roux can easily be doubled because it keeps well in the freezer or refrigerator. Today, some larger, regional grocery stores carry prepared roux in jars and the taste is excellent; it keeps very well in the refrigerator also.*

Basic Roux

In a heavy pot, combine 2 parts flour to 1 part vegetable oil. For a 5-quart pot, I recommend $2/3$ cup all-purpose flour and $1/3$ cup oil. Adjust amounts according to pot size. Cook over medium heat until the desired color is reached. Stir continuously.

No Fat Oven Roux

This is a great roux to keep on hand because you can add a spoonful or two to a soup or stew. Very convenient!

In a baking pan, spread 1 cup dry all-purpose flour evenly. Bake at 250 degrees for 2 to 4 hours, depending on the desired color (2 hours for a lighter color and 4 hours for a very dark color). Stir flour approximately every 30 minutes. Allow more baking time for larger batches.

Easy Microwave Roux

Mix $2/3$ cup all-purpose flour and $2/3$ cup vegetable oil in a microwave safe dish. Cook on high for approximately 7 minutes, stirring every 2 minutes. Cook until desired color is achieved. Transfer it to a gumbo pot. Add additional oil if the roux becomes too dry.

Seafood

FISH
Catfish Courtboullion 54 • Creole Baked Fish 55 • Blackened Redfish 55 • Favorite Fried Fish 56 • Crab and Shrimp Stuffed Flounder 56

CRAB
Crab and Shrimp Stuffing 57 • Easy Crab Bisque 57 • Stuffed Crab 58

CRAWFISH
Creamy Crawfish Casserole 58 • Crawfish au Gratin 59 • Rice Cooker Crawfish Jambalaya 60 • Easy Crawfish Fettucini 60 • Easy Crawfish Pie 61 • Boiled Crawfish 62 • Cajun Cornbread 62 • Crawfish Stuffed Bell Peppers 63

SHRIMP
Shrimp and Rice Casserole 64 • Fried Shrimp 64 • Stuffed Fried Shrimp 65 • Shrimp Creole 65 • Shrimp Étouffée 66 • Microwave Étouffée 66 • Shrimp Sauce Piquant 67 • Shrimp and Spinach Stuffed Bread 68

BASIC SEAFOODS
Grandma's Oyster and Chicken Dressing 69 • Seafood Casserole 70 • Easy Seafood Quiche 70 • Seafood Bake 71 • Seafood Stuffed Baked Tomatoes 72 • Seafood Stuffed Eggplant 73 • Seafood Lasagna 74 • Lurline's Seafood Spaghetti 75 • Seafood and Rice Salad 75 • Seafood Salad 76 • Seafood Gumbo 76 • Seafood Jambalaya 77

Center photo: I remember David Saizan declaring in the third grade that he was going to quit school to hunt and fish for the rest of his life. Today, David (who finished school) is a park ranger at Toledo Bend State Park in northern Louisiana. He is also an expert fisherman and hunter, living a "sportsman's dream" as did our father.

Clockwise from left to right: My dad, Jim Saizan. Chantelle Prejean's first crabbing trip. Lakeshore. Lurline Duplechain. Gary and Danny Prejean. Crawfish, ready to cook. Maque choux or fried corn.

Catfish Courtboullion

I acquired this recipe from a very old Cajun restaurant going out of business. It is very good!

3	POUNDS CATFISH FILLETS
$1/3$	CUP ALL-PURPOSE FLOUR
$1/3$	CUP VEGETABLE OIL
$1/2$	CUP ONION, CHOPPED
$1/2$	CUP BELL PEPPER, CHOPPED
$1/2$	CUP CELERY, CHOPPED
1	6-OUNCE CAN TOMATO PASTE
3	CANS WATER
1	TABLESPOON DRIED PARSLEY
$1/4$	CUP GREEN ONION, CHOPPED
1	TABLESPOON WORCESTERSHIRE SAUCE
$1^1/2$	TEASPOONS SALT
$1/4$	TEASPOON RED PEPPER
$1/4$	TEASPOON BLACK PEPPER
$1/2$	TEASPOON GARLIC POWDER
1	TEASPOON PAPRIKA
1	TABLESPOON GRANULATED SUGAR
	HOT COOKED RICE

Prepare and broil fish fillets. Set aside. In a heavy pot, combine flour and oil and cook until medium brown in color. Add remaining ingredients except fish. Simmer for approximately 30 minutes. Add cooked fish and simmer for another 30 minutes. Be careful when stirring not to break fish apart. Serve over rice. Yield: 10–12 servings.

Courtboullion, pronounced **coo-be-yon,** *is a fish stew made with vegetables, seasonings, and sometimes wine.*

Creole Baked Fish

8	SLICES OF BACON
$1^1/_2$–2	POUNDS OF YOUR FAVORITE TYPE OF FISH FILLETS
1	LEMON
$1/_2$	CUP MARGARINE OR BUTTER
$1/_2$	CUP ONION, CHOPPED
$1/_4$	CUP CELERY, CHOPPED
$1/_4$	CUP BELL PEPPER, CHOPPED
$1/_4$	CUP GREEN ONION, CHOPPED
$2/_3$	CUP TOMATO, CHOPPED
2	TABLESPOONS WORCESTERSHIRE SAUCE
1	BAY LEAF, CRUMBLED
1	TEASPOON CAJUN SEASONING

Preheat oven to 350 degrees. Arrange half the bacon in a baking dish. Place fillets on top. Cut lemon and squeeze juice liberally over fish. Place remaining bacon over fish. In a skillet over medium-low heat, melt margarine or butter and sauté chopped vegetables over medium-low heat until soft, approximately 5 to 10 minutes. Stir in remaining ingredients. Pour mixture over fish. Bake covered for 45 minutes. Yield: 6–8 servings.

Blackened Redfish

This recipe was contributed by my sister-in-law, Sondra Corbin Freitag. Sondra has been a New Orleans resident for over 25 years and this is one of the favorites she's added to her recipe collection.

1	POUND REDFISH FILLETS
$1/_2$	CUP MARGARINE OR BUTTER, MELTED
3	TEASPOONS CAJUN SEASONING
$1/_2$	TEASPOON THYME

Brush sides of fish liberally with margarine or butter. Sprinkle seasonings onto fish; do not overcoat. Place fillets in a medium-hot skillet that has been sprayed or coated with vegetable oil. Cook fillets until browned on both sides, approximately 2–3 minutes. This recipe can also be done outside on the grill by placing the skillet directly on the coals. Yield: 3–4 servings.

Favorite Fried Fish

This fried fish recipe comes from my younger brother, David Saizan. David has been a fisherman ever since he could cast a line and an outdoorsman ever since he was allowed outdoors. I can remember David catching crawfish from the front yard ditch for his supper one night when we were children. A true Cajun!

2–3	POUNDS ANY FISH FILLETS
	CAJUN SEASONING TO TASTE
1	BOX CORN FLAKES
2	EGGS, BEATEN
$^1/_4$	CUP WATER
	VEGETABLE OIL FOR FRYING

Season fillets with Cajun seasoning. Pulverize 1 box of corn flakes in blender until powder. Place corn flake powder in zippered bag. In a bowl, beat together eggs and water. Dip fillets in egg mixture and then in zippered bag. Fry fillets in an inch or so of oil on medium-high heat for 2–3 minutes or until golden brown. Drain on paper towels. Yield: 10–12 fish fillets or 5–6 servings.

Crab and Shrimp Stuffed Flounder

This delicious flounder dish was often prepared by my parents. My father, an excellent Cajun cook, and my mother, an excellent southern cook, created this recipe. Their crab and shrimp stuffing is about the best I've ever run across. Absolutely delicious!

1	LARGE (2- TO 3-POUND) FLOUNDER
1	LEMON
	SALT AND PEPPER TO TASTE
	BUTTER TO TASTE

Preheat oven to 350 degrees. Prepare and butterfly fish. Squeeze lemon juice liberally inside and out. Salt and pepper fish lightly, inside and out. Stuff Crab and Shrimp Stuffing into cavity (see recipe on facing page). Seal edges with toothpicks. Dot outside of fish with butter. Place in a covered dish and bake for 40 to 45 minutes. Yield: 6–8 servings.

Crab and Shrimp Stuffing

$1/2$	POUND SMALL SHRIMP
$1/2$	CUP COOKED OR 1 6-OUNCE CAN CRABMEAT, DRAINED
$1/2$	CUP MARGARINE OR BUTTER
$1/2$	CUP ONION, CHOPPED
2	EGGS, BEATEN
3	BREAD SLICES
$1/4$	CUP GREEN ONION, CHOPPED
$1/2$	CUP CELERY, CHOPPED
2	TABLESPOONS BELL PEPPER, CHOPPED
$1/4$	CUP DRIED PARSLEY FLAKES
	SALT AND PEPPER TO TASTE

Peel small shrimp. Boil in salted water. Drain and chop finely. Mix with the crabmeat. Set aside. In a skillet over medium-low heat, sauté onion and margarine or butter until soft. Combine with shrimp and crab mixture. In a small bowl, soak bread slices in the beaten eggs until absorbed. Add to shrimp and crab mixture along with all remaining ingredients. Mix well. Taste if necessary to adjust seasonings. Spoon mixture into split fish. Seal edges with toothpicks. Yield: 8 $1/2$-cup servings.

Easy Crab Bisque

1	$10^1/_2$-OUNCE CAN CREAM OF MUSHROOM SOUP
1	$10^1/_2$-OUNCE CAN CREAM OF ASPARAGUS SOUP
1	CUP WHOLE MILK
1	CUP LIGHT CREAM
$1/2$	CUP COOKED OR 1 6-OUNCE CAN CRABMEAT, DRAINED

In a pot, combine soups. Stir in milk and cream. Add the crabmeat and bring to a boil. Serve warm with a pat of butter or a sprinkling of cheese. Perfect! Yield: 4–5 servings.

Stuffed Crab

$3/4$ POUND COOKED OR 3 6-OUNCE CANS CRABMEAT, DRAINED
$1/2$ CUP MARGARINE OR BUTTER
$1/2$ CUP ONION, CHOPPED
$1/2$ CUP CELERY, CHOPPED
2   EGGS, BEATEN
3   BREAD SLICES
$1/4$ CUP GREEN ONION, CHOPPED
$1/4$ CUP PARSLEY FLAKES
     SALT AND PEPPER TO TASTE

Preheat oven to 350 degrees. If using fresh crabs, boil in seasoned water. Drain and remove crabmeat. Clean shells thoroughly. Set aside. If using canned crab, aluminum crab shells can be purchased. In skillet over medium-low heat, sauté onion and celery in margarine or butter. Meanwhile, soak bread in beaten eggs. Add cooked vegetables and crabmeat to the skillet. Stir in remaining ingredients and season to taste. Spoon mixture in crabshells. Bake for 25 minutes or until tops begin to brown. Fills approximately 8 crabshells.

Creamy Crawfish Casserole

1   POUND COOKED CRAWFISH TAILS, PEELED AND RINSED
$1/2$ CUP MARGARINE OR BUTTER
$1/2$ CUP ONION, CHOPPED
$1/2$ CUP CELERY, CHOPPED
1   3-OUNCE PACKAGE CREAM CHEESE
1    $10^1/_2$-OUNCE CAN CREAM OF MUSHROOM SOUP
$1/2$ CUP WHOLE MILK
$1/2$ TEASPOON SALT
$1/2$ TEASPOON RED PEPPER
$1/4$ TEASPOON BLACK PEPPER
3   CUPS RICE, COOKED
1   CUP CHEDDAR CHEESE, GRATED

Preheat oven to 350 degrees. Melt margarine or butter in a skillet. Sauté chopped vegetables over medium-low heat until soft. Sir in crawfish tails and add cream cheese, soup, and milk. Cook until cream cheese melts and the mixture is well blended. Stir in remaining ingredients and pour into a casserole dish. Sprinkle grated cheese on top. Bake uncovered for 30 minutes. Yield: 8–10 servings.

The crawfish is a relative of the lobster, found almost everywhere in the world. There are over five hundred species of crawfish with a life span from one to twenty years depending on the species. Found in freshwater creeks, a great deal of the nation's commercially harvested crawfish come from Louisiana.

Crawfish Au Gratin

The next two crawfish recipes have been contributed by Joyce Rodrigue. Crawfish Au Gratin and Crawfish Rice Cooker Jambalaya are both excellent and well worth trying!

$1/2$	CUP ONION, CHOPPED
1	CUP BELL PEPPER, CHOPPED
3	GARLIC CLOVES, MINCED
$1^1/2$	CUPS GREEN ONION, CHOPPED
$1/2$	CUP MARGARINE OR BUTTER, MELTED
1	2-OUNCE JAR PIMENTOS, DRAINED
2	TABLESPOONS ALL-PURPOSE FLOUR
1	10-OUNCE PACKAGE CHEDDAR CHEESE, SHREDDED
1	12-OUNCE CAN EVAPORATED MILK
1	TEASPOON CAJUN SEASONING
2	POUNDS COOKED CRAWFISH TAILS, PEELED AND RINSED

Preheat oven to 350 degrees. In a skillet over medium-low heat, sauté vegetables in margarine or butter until tender. Stir in flour. Stir in half of the cheese and half the milk, until a creamy consistency is reached. Stir in the remaining milk and spices, and finally the crawfish. Pour into a casserole dish and sprinkle with remaining cheese. Bake for 30 minutes or until hot and bubbly. Yield: 8–10 servings.

Rice Cooker Crawfish Jambalaya

2   CUPS RICE, UNCOOKED
2   POUNDS COOKED CRAWFISH TAILS, PEELED AND RINSED
1   10-OUNCE CAN TOMATOES WITH CHILI PEPPERS
1   10-OUNCE CAN BEEF BROTH
1   4-OUNCE CAN MUSHROOMS, DRAINED
1   CUP ONION, CHOPPED
1   CUP BELL PEPPER, CHOPPED
$1/2$ CUP GREEN ONION, CHOPPED
1   TEASPOON CAJUN SEASONING
1   STICK MARGARINE OR BUTTER, MELTED

Mix all ingredients except margarine or butter and pour into rice cooker. Pour melted margarine or butter over mixture. Cover and cook as you would rice. Allow mixture to steam for an additional 30 minutes. This recipe may also be cooked in the microwave. Cover and cook for 20 minutes, rotating after 10 minutes. Yield: 10–12 servings.

Easy Crawfish Fettucini

My cousin Lurline Rodrigue Duplechain contributed the next two crawfish recipes. Easy Crawfish Fettuccini and Easy Crawfish Pie are absolutely delicious and well worth trying!

1   POUND COOKED CRAWFISH TAILS, PEELED AND RINSED
$1/2$ CUP MARGARINE OR BUTTER
$1/4$ CUP CELERY, CHOPPED
$1/4$ CUP BELL PEPPER, CHOPPED
$1/2$ CUP ONION, CHOPPED
3   TABLESPOONS ALL-PURPOSE FLOUR
1   8-OUNCE JAR AMERICAN CHEESESPREAD
$1/2$ PINT HALF AND HALF
2   TABLESPOONS PARSLEY
1   TEASPOON CAJUN SEASONING
8   OUNCES FETTUCINI NOODLES, COOKED

In a large skillet, melt margarine or butter. Sauté chopped vegetables over medium-low heat until soft. Stir in crawfish tails. Add flour and cook until golden brown. Add remaining ingredients and continue cooking until cheese has melted and the mixture is well blended. Cover and cook over low heat for an additional 15 minutes. Add cooked noodles. Toss well to coat noodles. Yield: 4–6 servings.

Easy Crawfish Pie

1	CUP ONION, CHOPPED
$1/_2$	CUP CELERY, CHOPPED
$1/_2$	CUP BELL PEPPER, CHOPPED
$1^1/_2$	CUPS GREEN ONION, CHOPPED
$1/_2$	CUP MARGARINE OR BUTTER
1	$10^1/_2$-OUNCE CAN CREAM OF MUSHROOM SOUP
1	$10^1/_2$-OUNCE CAN CREAM OF CELERY SOUP
	RED PEPPER FLAKES
	SALT AND PEPPER TO TASTE
1	POUND COOKED CRAWFISH TAILS, PEELED AND RINSED
1	CUP RICE, COOKED
	PASTRY FOR TOP

Preheat oven to 350 degrees. In a skillet over medium-low heat, sauté vegetables in margarine or butter until wilted. Stir in soups and seasonings and heat through. Stir in crawfish tails and rice. Add a little milk or water if consistency is too thick. Pour mixture into greased casserole dish. Top with your favorite piecrust. Make slits on top of crust. Bake for 30 minutes. This recipe can also be made with a prepared pie shell on the bottom and then sealed with the second crust on top. Yield: 8 servings.

Crawfish wasn't the only thing boiled in large pots. Every fall, my ancestors had a rusty-nail boil. They would round up rusty nails and boil them in a large cast-iron pot. The entire family would then drink the liquid for their annual "iron supply." This custom was passed down from generation to generation, stopping sometime before my generation, since I don't recall such an event. Little did my ancestors know that they were already getting their iron supply from the foods being cooked in the cast-iron pots.

Boiled Crawfish

25	POUNDS LIVE CRAWFISH
1	CUP EPSOM SALTS
5	POUNDS NEW POTATOES
$2^1/_2$	POUNDS MINI CORN ON THE COB, FROZEN
7	OUNCES CAJUN SEASONING
26	OUNCES TABLE SALT
$1^1/_2$	OUNCES BLACK PEPPER
	PLENTY OF NEWSPAPERS
	COCKTAIL SAUCE
1	LARGE POT AND METAL BASKET
	OUTDOOR BURNER

Purge crawfish in sink by soaking in Epsom salts dissolved in a sink full of water. Outside, prepare burner. Fill large pot with water. Place over burner. When water boils, add the potatoes, corn, and seasonings into pot basket. Return to boil and continue cooking for 15 minutes. Drop the crawfish into the basket. Cover and cook for an additional 10 minutes. Bring basket up and drain. Empty the basket onto spread newspapers. Serve with cocktail sauce or lemon and butter for dipping. Plan on 5 to 8 pounds of crawfish per person. Shrimp can also be cooked by this method. Allow 1 to 2 pounds of shrimp per person. See page 5 for Homemade Cocktail Sauce. Yield: 5–8 servings.

Cajun Cornbread

1	POUND COOKED CRAWFISH TAILS, PEELED AND RINSED
$1/_2$	CUP ONION, CHOPPED
2	JALAPEÑO PEPPERS, CHOPPED
$1/_3$	CUP BELL PEPPER, CHOPPED
2	TABLESPOONS MARGARINE OR BUTTER
1	CUP YELLOW CORNMEAL
1	$15^1/_2$-OUNCE CAN CREAM CORN
1	CUP WHOLE MILK
$1/_4$	CUP VEGETABLE OIL
1	TEASPOON CAJUN SEASONING
$1/_2$	TEASPOON BAKING SODA
$1^1/_2$	CUPS CHEDDAR CHEESE, GRATED

Preheat oven to 375 degrees. In a skillet over medium-low heat, sauté onion, bell pepper, and jalapeño peppers in margarine or butter until soft. Stir in crawfish and set aside. In a large bowl, mix remaining ingredients except cheese; stir well. Coat a large skillet with oil or vegetable spray and heat to medium-high. Pour half of the cornbread batter into skillet, then add crawfish-vegetable mixture. Sprinkle cheese on top, and pour the remaining cornbread batter on top. Remove from stovetop and bake at 375 degrees for 1 hour. Cool before cutting. Yield: 8 servings.

Crawfish Stuffed Bell Peppers

$1/2$	POUND CRAWFISH TAILS, PEELED AND RINSED
5	BELL PEPPER
$1/4$	CUP MARGARINE OR BUTTER
$1/2$	CUP ONION, CHOPPED
$1/4$	CUP CELERY, CHOPPED
1	EGG
$1/2$	CUP PLAIN BREAD CRUMBS
1	8-OUNCE CAN TOMATO SAUCE
$1/2$	10-OUNCE CAN TOMATOES WITH CHILI PEPPERS
2	CUPS RICE, COOKED
1	TABLESPOON WORCESTERSHIRE SAUCE
$1/2$	TEASPOON SALT
	DASH OF GARLIC POWDER
$1/4$	TEASPOON BLACK PEPPER
1	TEASPOON PARSLEY
	PARMESAN CHEESE

Preheat oven to 350 degrees. Prepare the peppers for stuffing. Set aside. In a small skillet, melt margarine or butter. Sauté onion and celery over medium-low heat until soft. In a large mixing bowl, beat egg. Add bread crumbs, $1/2$ the can of tomato sauce, and the remaining ingredients except the Parmesan cheese. Stir in the sautéed vegetables. Mix well. Spoon mixture into peppers. Add water to the remaining tomato sauce to equal a full can. Stir well. Pour on top of peppers and sprinkle Parmesan cheese on top. Cover and bake for approximately 40 minutes. Shrimp may be substituted for the crawfish. Yield: 5 servings.

Shrimp and Rice Casserole

$^1/_2$	CUP COOKING OIL
2	TABLESPOONS ALL-PURPOSE FLOUR
$1^1/_2$	CUPS ONION, CHOPPED
$^1/_8$	TEASPOON GARLIC JUICE
$^1/_4$	CUP BELL PEPPER, CHOPPED
1	15-OUNCE CAN TOMATOES
2	CUPS WATER, DIVIDED
2	CUPS RAW SHRIMP, PEELED AND DEVEINED
$^1/_4$	CUP GREEN ONION, CHOPPED
2	TABLESPOONS PARSLEY FLAKES
1	$10^1/_2$-OUNCE CAN CREAM OF MUSHROOM SOUP
3	CUPS RICE, COOKED
	SALT AND PEPPER TO TASTE

Preheat oven to 350 degrees. In a large skillet, cook oil and flour over medium heat stirring continuously until golden brown. Add onion, garlic juice, bell pepper, tomatoes, and 1 cup water. Cook until onion are tender. Add remaining water and bring to a boil. Add shrimp, green onion, parsley, and soup. Cook over medium heat for approximately 5 minutes or until the shrimp turn pink. Remove from heat. Stir in rice, salt, and pepper. Pour into a casserole dish and bake for 30 minutes. Yield: 8–10 servings.

Fried Shrimp

1	POUND FRESH SHRIMP
	SALT AND PEPPER TO TASTE
1	EGG, BEATEN
3	TABLESPOONS WATER
$1^1/_2$	CUPS DRY BISCUIT OR PANCAKE MIX
	OIL FOR FRYING

Peel and devein shrimp and season to taste. In a bowl, make an egg wash with the beaten egg and water. Dip shrimp into the egg mixture and then into the dry biscuit mix. Fry in hot oil until golden brown. Drain on paper towels. Serve with Homemade Cocktail Sauce (see p. 5). Crawfish, oysters, and fish are also excellent using this method. Yield: 3–5 servings.

Stuffed Fried Shrimp

1	POUND LARGE SHRIMP
	SALT AND PEPPER TO TASTE
4	CUPS OF CRAB AND SHRIMP STUFFING (SEE P. 57)
1	SMALL BOWL OF ALL-PURPOSE FLOUR
1	BOWL WITH 2 EGGS, BEATEN AND 4 TABLESPOONS WATER
1	BOWL CONTAINING 2 CUPS PLAIN BREAD CRUMBS
	OIL FOR FRYING

Peel and devein the shrimp. Cut lengthwise, but do not cut in half. Salt and pepper to taste. Place approximately 1 tablespoon of the stuffing into the split side of each shrimp. Place shrimp in flour, then egg, and finally bread crumbs. Fry in medium to hot oil until golden brown. Yield: 4–6 servings.

Shrimp Creole

Shrimp Creole and Shrimp Étouffée are family favorites that my mother often made, and which my daughters and I now cook. Both are excellent.

3	TABLESPOONS VEGETABLE OIL
$1/2$	CUP ONION, CHOPPED
$1/2$	CUP CELERY, CHOPPED
1	CLOVE GARLIC, MINCED
1	TABLESPOON ALL-PURPOSE FLOUR
1	CUP WATER
1	15-OUNCE CAN TOMATOES, CHOPPED
1	8-OUNCE CAN TOMATO SAUCE
1	TEASPOON RED HOT SAUCE
1	TABLESPOON WORCESTERSHIRE SAUCE
1	TEASPOON GRANULATED SUGAR
1	TEASPOON SALT
$1/4$	TEASPOON BLACK PEPPER
1	POUND SHRIMP, PEELED AND DEVEINED
	HOT COOKED RICE

In a large skillet over medium-low heat, sauté onion, celery, and garlic in oil. Stir in flour and cook until golden. Add remaining ingredients except shrimp and rice. Cover and cook over low heat for 30 minutes. Add the shrimp and continue for an additional 15 minutes. Serve over hot rice. Yield: 6–8 servings.

Shrimp Étouffée

$^1/_2$	CUP MARGARINE OR BUTTER
$^2/_3$	CUP CELERY, CHOPPED
$^2/_3$	CUP ONION, CHOPPED
$^1/_3$	CUP BELL PEPPER, CHOPPED
$^1/_3$	CUP GREEN ONION, CHOPPED
$1^1/_2$	TEASPOONS PAPRIKA
3	TABLESPOONS ALL-PURPOSE FLOUR
2	CUPS WATER
$^1/_4$	TEASPOON BLACK PEPPER
$^3/_8$	TEASPOON GARLIC POWDER
$^3/_8$	TEASPOON SALT OR TO TASTE
1	TEASPOON RED HOT SAUCE (OR TO TASTE)
1	POUND SHRIMP, PEELED AND DEVEINED
	HOT COOKED RICE

In a large saucepan over medium-low heat, sauté vegetables in margarine or butter until tender. Stir in flour and paprika; continue cooking until golden in color. Stir in water and spices. Simmer for 20 minutes. Add shrimp and continue to simmer for another 20 minutes. Adjust seasonings if necessary. Serve over hot rice. Yield: 6–8 servings. Crawfish can be used in place of shrimp.

Microwave Étouffée

As time passes and people change, so do their recipes. With the invention of the microwave and the help of canned soups, smart cooks realized that Cajun cooking could be simplified. My sister-in-law Sheri Corbin Brock is a Sulphur, Louisiana, native and contributed this recipe.

$^1/_4$	CUP MARGARINE OR BUTTER
$^2/_3$	CUP ONION, CHOPPED
$^2/_3$	CUP CELERY, CHOPPED
$^1/_3$	CUP BELL PEPPER, CHOPPED
$^1/_3$	CUP GREEN ONION, CHOPPED
2	$10^1/_2$-OUNCE CANS CREAM OF MUSHROOM SOUP
1	10-OUNCE CAN TOMATOES WITH CHILI PEPPERS
1	POUND SHRIMP, PEELED AND DEVEINED
	HOT COOKED RICE

In a microwave dish, sauté raw vegetables in margarine or butter until soft, approximately 5 minutes. Stir in remaining ingredients and microwave on high for 5 minutes, stirring halfway through. Cream of celery soup can be substituted for the mushroom soup. Serve over hot rice. Yield: 6–8 servings. Crawfish can be used in place of shrimp.

Shrimp Sauce Piquant

This sauce recipe was taught to my mother-in-law, Nell Williams Corbin, by a neighbor who happened to be an excellent Cajun cook. Having just moved to Abbeville, Louisiana, from Alabama, Nell learned a lot of Cajun-cooking pointers from her neighbors.

$1/4$	CUP VEGETABLE OIL
$1/2$	CUP ALL-PURPOSE FLOUR
1	CUP ONION, CHOPPED
$3/4$	CUP BELL PEPPER, CHOPPED
1	CUP CELERY, CHOPPED
1	6-OUNCE CAN TOMATO PASTE
1	10-OUNCE CAN TOMATOES WITH CHILI PEPPERS
2	CUPS WATER
$1/2$	TEASPOON SALT
1	TEASPOON GARLIC POWDER
1	TABLESPOON GRANULATED SUGAR
1	TABLESPOON WORCESTERSHIRE SAUCE
1	POUND SHRIMP, PEELED AND DEVEINED
$1/2$	LEMON, THINLY SLICED
	HOT COOKED RICE

Make a roux with the oil and flour, cooking over medium heat, stirring continuously until medium brown (see p. 50). Add vegetables to the roux and cook until soft. Stir in the remaining ingredients except lemons. Simmer for approximately 20 minutes. Add the lemon slices for the last 5 minutes for that piquant or tart flavor. If the flavor is too tart for your liking, add a little sugar to cut the tartness. Serve over rice. Yield: 6–8 servings. Crawfish can be used instead of shrimp.

There are over two thousand species of shrimp. The more common commercial varieties are the brown, white gulf, and rock varieties. Shrimp can be kept in the freezer for up to 6 months and in the refrigerator for only a day or two. The gritty vein running on the back side of the shrimp is usually removed before cooking, however it is harmless if eaten in cooked shrimp.

Shrimp and Spinach Stuffed Bread

My cousin Susan Thibodeaux Betancourt, a Baton Rouge, Louisiana, native and a full-time working mother, has contributed this easy and unique bread. It can be served as a main course or cut into small pieces and served as an appetizer.

1	LOAF OF FRENCH BREAD, SPLIT AND HOLLOWED
1	PACKAGE FROZEN SPINACH, CHOPPED
$^1/_2$	CUP MARGARINE OR BUTTER
2	TABLESPOONS ONION, CHOPPED
1	CLOVE GARLIC, MINCED
1	CUP SHRIMP, PEELED AND DEVEINED
1	TEASPOON CAJUN SEASONING
1	CUP CHEDDAR CHEESE, SHREDDED
1	CUP MOZZARELLA CHEESE, SHREDDED

Preheat oven to 400 degrees. Cook spinach in salted water. Drain thoroughly and blot excess water with paper towels. While spinach is cooking, sauté onion and garlic in margarine or butter over medium-low heat until soft. Add shrimp and continue cooking until the shrimp are pink. Stir in spinach, cajun seasoning, and cheddar cheese. Spoon mixture into hollowed French bread halves. Sprinkle remaining cheese on top. Bake for 20 minutes. Yield: 8–10 main course servings or 16–20 appetizers.

Grandma's Oyster and Chicken Dressing

This oyster dressing was served quite often at holidays or on special occasions. My grandmother Robertha Rodrigue Saizan enjoyed cooking this dish. I remember this as one of her specialties.

3–4	CHICKEN PIECES
1	CUP ONION, CHOPPED
2	GARLIC CLOVES, MINCED
1	PINT OYSTERS, DRAINED
1	CUP GREEN ONION, CHOPPED
1	TEASPOON SALT
$1/2$	TEASPOON RED PEPPER
$1/2$	TEASPOON BLACK PEPPER
3	CUPS RICE, COOKED

In a pot, cover chicken pieces with water. Add chopped onion and garlic. Boil for an hour or until tender. Remove chicken, then debone and chop. Reserve 1–2 cups chicken broth with vegetables. In a mixing bowl, combine chicken, oysters, green onion, seasonings, and cooked rice. Add enough reserved broth to moisten the dressing. Serve as a side dish or use as stuffing for a turkey or goose. Yield: 10–12 servings.

In the early 1900s, oysters were so plentiful they were two to three feet deep in the river and lake bottoms along the Louisiana Gulf Coast. The bottoms were dredged by draglines to deepen and widen the waterways for ships to travel on. Oysters were not only used as food, but the shells were used commercially in place of limestone or gravel.

Seafood Casserole

$3/4$	CUP MARGARINE OR BUTTER
$1^1/_2$	CUPS ONION, CHOPPED
$1/_2$	CUP BELL PEPPER, CHOPPED
$1/_2$	CUP CELERY, CHOPPED
1	4-OUNCE CAN MUSHROOMS, DRAINED
1	8-OUNCE PACKAGE CREAM CHEESE
1	$10^1/_2$-OUNCE CAN CREAM OF MUSHROOM SOUP
1	CUP RICE, COOKED
1	POUND SHRIMP, PEELED AND DEVEINED
$1/_2$	POUND COOKED OR 2 6-OUNCE CANS CRABMEAT, DRAINED
1	TEASPOON RED HOT SAUCE, OR TO TASTE
$1/_2$	TEASPOON RED PEPPER
$1/_2$	TEASPOON SALT
1	CUP CRACKER CRUMBS
1	CUP CHEDDAR CHEESE, GRATED

Preheat oven to 350 degrees. In a skillet, melt margarine or butter. Sauté chopped vegetables over medium-low heat until soft. Add mushrooms and cubed cream cheese. Cook until melted. Stir in soup, rice, seafood, and seasonings. Pour into a medium-size casserole dish and top with cracker crumbs. Bake for approximately 20 minutes. Remove and add grated cheese; bake an additional 10 minutes or until cheese melts. Yield: 10–12 servings.

Easy Seafood Quiche

2	PREPARED PIECRUSTS
2	EGGS, BEATEN
2	TABLESPOONS CANNED PARMESAN CHEESE
2	TABLESPOONS GREEN ONION, CHOPPED
2	TABLESPOONS PLAIN BREAD CRUMBS
$1/_2$	TEASPOON DRIED PARSLEY
1	TEASPOON RED HOT SAUCE, OR TO TASTE
$1/_2$	TEASPOON SALT
$1/_2$	POUND FRESH OR 2 6-OUNCE CANS SEAFOOD, DRAINED
2	CUPS CHEDDAR CHEESE, GRATED

Preheat oven to 325 degrees. In a mixing bowl, combine beaten eggs, Parmesan cheese, onion, and remaining seasonings. Stir in bread crumbs, seafood, and grated cheese. Pour into pie shell. Cover mixture with remaining crust. Seal edges. Bake for 50 to 55 minutes or until a toothpick inserted comes out clean and crust is browned. Fresh shrimp and crab are excellent in this recipe! Yield: 8 servings.

Seafood Bake

$1/4$	CUP MARGARINE OR BUTTER
$1/2$	CUP CELERY, CHOPPED
$1/4$	CUP BELL PEPPER, CHOPPED
2	TABLESPOONS ONION, MINCED
$1/2$	CUP MAYONNAISE
3	OUNCES CREAM CHEESE, SOFTENED
$1/2$	TEASPOON RED PEPPER
$1/2$	TEASPOON SALT
1	CUP SHRIMP, PEELED AND DEVEINED
$1/2$	CUP COOKED OR 1 6-OUNCE CAN CRABMEAT, DRAINED
$1/4$	CUP MARGARINE OR BUTTER, MELTED
1	CUP PLAIN BREAD CRUMBS

Preheat oven to 350 degrees. In a skillet over medium-low heat, sauté celery, bell pepper, and onion in margarine or butter. Remove from heat and cool. In a mixing bowl, combine mayonnaise, softened cream cheese, seasonings, and seafood. Stir in sautéed vegetables. Spread into a medium-size casserole dish and sprinkle with the bread crumbs and melted margarine or butter. Bake for approximately 25 minutes or until heated through. Cool before serving. Yield: 4–6 servings.

Seafood Stuffed Baked Tomatoes

5–6	LARGE TOMATOES
$1/4$	CUP MARGARINE OR BUTTER
$1/2$	CUP ONION, CHOPPED
1	CUP CELERY, CHOPPED
$1/2$	CUP BELL PEPPER, CHOPPED
1	CUP SHRIMP, COOKED AND CHOPPED
3–4	SLICES BACON, COOKED AND CRUMBLED
1	SLEEVE OF BUTTER CRACKERS, CRUSHED
$1/4$	CUP CANNED PARMESAN CHEESE
$1/4$	TEASPOON RED PEPPER
$1/4$	TEASPOON BLACK PEPPER
$1/2$	TEASPOON SALT

Preheat oven to 400 degrees. Melt margarine or butter in a skillet. Cut off tops of the tomatoes. Scoop out the middle of the tomatoes and place in the skillet; set aside the tomato shells. Add chopped vegetables to skillet and sauté over medium-low heat until vegetables are soft. Stir in shrimp and crumbled bacon. Meanwhile, combine crushed crackers and Parmesan cheese, reserving $1/4$ cup. Add this to the vegetable and bacon mixture. Stir in seasonings. Spoon mixture into tomato shells and sprinkle with remaining $1/4$ cup cracker and cheese mixture. Bake for 15 minutes or until tops are browned. Yield: 5–6 servings.

There are over 4500 species of crab living in water and on land. A 3-ounce serving of crab contains only 74 calories, with 15 grams of protein and 1 gram of fat and a healthy dose of omega-3 fatty acids.

Seafood Stuffed Eggplant

Recipe provided by Lurline Duplechain.

3	MEDIUM EGGPLANTS
2	CUPS WATER
1	TEASPOON SALT
2	TABLESPOONS MARGARINE OR BUTTER
$1/2$	CUP CELERY, CHOPPED
$1/2$	CUP GREEN ONION, CHOPPED
$1/4$	CUP PARSLEY, CHOPPED
$1/4$	CUP BELL PEPPER, CHOPPED
2	CUPS RICE, COOKED
1	POUND SMALL SHRIMP, PEELED AND DEVEINED
2	CUPS COOKED OR 4 6-OUNCE CANS CRABMEAT, DRAINED
1	TEASPOON WORCESTERSHIRE SAUCE
$1/2$	TEASPOON OF SALT AND PEPPER
$1/2$	TEASPOON THYME

Preheat oven to 375 degrees. Halve each eggplant and scoop out the center; set scooped eggplant aside. In a large saucepan, combine water and salt, and parboil the eggplant shells for 5 minutes. Drain. Meanwhile, melt margarine or butter in a large skillet and sauté vegetables over medium-low heat including the eggplant centers. Add remaining ingredients and heat for 5 minutes stirring continuously. Spoon mixture into eggplant halves and bake for 25 minutes. This recipe can easily be halved. Yield: 6 servings.

Seafood Lasagna

1	12-OUNCE PACKAGE LASAGNA NOODLES
$1/3$	CUP MARGARINE OR BUTTER
$1/2$	CUP ONION, CHOPPED
$1/2$	CUP BELL PEPPER, CHOPPED
1	GARLIC CLOVE, MINCED
2	TABLESPOON PARSLEY FLAKES
2	CUPS WATER
1	CUP CRAWFISH TAILS, COOKED AND RINSED
1	CUP SHRIMP, PEELED AND DEVEINED
1	$15^{1}/_{2}$-OUNCE CAN TOMATOES, CHOPPED
1	8-OUNCE CAN TOMATO SAUCE
1	TABLESPOON RED HOT SAUCE
1	TABLESPOON WORCESTERSHIRE SAUCE
1	TEASPOON CAJUN SEASONING
$1/4$	TEASPOON BLACK PEPPER
1	8-OUNCE CARTON RICOTTA OR COTTAGE CHEESE
1	12-OUNCE PACKAGE GRATED MOZZARELLA CHEESE

Cook lasagna noodles. Drain. Preheat oven to 350 degrees. In a large skillet over medium-low heat, sauté onion, bell pepper, and garlic in margarine or butter. Add remaining ingredients except cheeses. Simmer until shrimp turn pink. In a greased casserole dish, spread a thin layer of noodles, followed by ricotta cheese, seafood sauce, and shredded cheese. Repeat layers until all ingredients are gone. Bake for 45 minutes. Yield: 15–18 servings.

Lurline's Seafood Spaghetti

3	TABLESPOONS COOKING OIL
1	10-OUNCE CAN TOMATOES WITH CHILI PEPPERS
$1/4$	CUP ONION, CHOPPED
$1/4$	CUP GREEN ONION, CHOPPED
$1/4$	CUP BELL PEPPER, CHOPPED
$1/4$	CUP FRESH PARSLEY, CHOPPED
1	$10^1/_2$-OUNCE CAN MUSHROOM SOUP
3	CUPS WATER
2	TEASPOONS CAJUN SEASONING
	DASH OF GARLIC POWDER
$1/2$	POUND COOKED OR 2 6-OUNCE CANS CRABMEAT, DRAINED
2	POUNDS SHRIMP, PEELED AND DEVEINED
1	16-OUNCE PACKAGE SPAGHETTI

In a large pot over medium-low heat, cook tomatoes and chopped vegetables in oil until tomatoes begin to brown. Add soup, water, and the remaining ingredients except spaghetti. Bring to a boil, then reduce to low heat. Meanwhile, in another pot parboil spaghetti for approximately 3 minutes and drain. Add to sauce and continue cooking over low heat until spaghetti is tender. Yield: 10–12 servings.

Seafood and Rice Salad

2	CUPS RICE, COOKED
$1/2$	CUP MAYONNAISE
$1/4$	CUP SWEET PICKLE RELISH
2	TABLESPOONS GREEN ONION, CHOPPED
$1/4$	CUP CELERY, CHOPPED
$1/2$	POUND SHRIMP, PEELED AND COOKED
$1/2$	CUP COOKED OR 1 6-OUNCE CAN CRABMEAT, DRAINED
1	TEASPOON CAJUN SEASONING OR TO TASTE

Mix all ingredients together. Chill on a bed of lettuce leaves. Serve cold with cajun crackers (see p. 14). Yield: 5 cups salad.

Seafood Salad

8	OUNCES FRESH OR 2 6-OUNCE CANS SEAFOOD, DRAINED
1/3	CUP MAYONNAISE
1/4	CUP CELERY, CHOPPED
2	TABLESPOONS GREEN ONION
1	TEASPOON FRESH PARSLEY, CHOPPED
1	TEASPOON WORCESTERSHIRE SAUCE
1	TABLESPOON LEMON JUICE
1/2	TEASPOON CAJUN SEASONING OR TO TASTE

Mix all ingredients. Chill and serve on a bed of lettuce leaves with tomato wedges and boiled eggs quarters if desired. Crab and shrimp are best in this recipe. Yield: 2 cups salad.

Seafood Gumbo

This seafood gumbo recipe was sent to me by my friend Danny Gentry. He says he's a hillbilly turned Cajun. Originally from Arkansas, Danny has lived in Louisiana for the past twenty-five years and has picked up most of his Cajun techniques from my father. This is the best seafood gumbo I've ever eaten.

1	CUP ALL-PURPOSE FLOUR
2/3	CUP OIL
2	CUPS ONION, CHOPPED
1 1/2	CUPS BELL PEPPER, CHOPPED
2/3	CUP CELERY, CHOPPED
4	GARLIC CLOVES, CHOPPED
8	CUPS WATER
	WORCESTERSHIRE SAUCE, TO TASTE
	SALT AND PEPPER, TO TASTE
1	BUNCH GREEN ONION, CHOPPED
1	SMALL BUNCH PARSLEY, CHOPPED
2	POUNDS SHRIMP, PEELED AND DEVEINED
2	CUPS CRABMEAT, COOKED
2	CUPS OYSTERS, DRAINED

In a very large gumbo pot, combine the flour and oil. Cook over medium heat until medium brown, stirring continuously. Add the chopped onion, bell pepper, celery, and garlic. Continue cooking until soft. Add approximately 8 cups of water and the seasonings. Cook over medium heat for 1 hour. Add the parsley and green onion; cook an additional 15 minutes. Add seafoods and cook for another 15 minutes. Serve with filé and hot sauce over hot rice. Yield: 18–22 servings.

Seafood Jambalaya

$^1/_2$	CUP MARGARINE OR BUTTER
1	CUP ONION, CHOPPED
$^1/_2$	CUP CELERY, CHOPPED
$^1/_4$	CUP BELL PEPPER, CHOPPED
$^1/_4$	CUP GREEN ONION, CHOPPED
2	TABLESPOONS ALL-PURPOSE FLOUR
3	OUNCES TOMATO PASTE
1	2-OUNCE JAR PIMENTOS, DRAINED
1	4-OUNCE CAN MUSHROOMS, DRAINED
$2^1/_2$	CUPS WATER
1	CUP RICE, UNCOOKED
1	TEASPOON SALT
$^1/_2$	TEASPOON RED PEPPER
$^1/_4$	TEASPOON DRIED PARSLEY
1	POUND SHRIMP, PEELED AND DEVEINED
1	POUND CRAWFISH TAILS, PEELED AND RINSED

In a large pot over medium-low heat, sauté chopped vegetables in melted margarine or butter until soft. Stir in flour and tomato paste. Add pimentos and mushrooms. Slowly stir in water until well blended. Add rice and seasonings, stirring well. Add seafood. Reduce heat to simmer and cover. Cook for approximately 30 minutes or until all water is absorbed. Serve with hot sauce if desired. Yield: 10–12 servings.

Wild Game, Poultry, & Meats

Venison Jerky 80 • Bacon Stuffed Venison 80 • Venison Sausage 81 • Venison Marinade 81 • Fried Venison Steaks 82 • Chicken and Andouille Gumbo 82 • Okra Gumbo 83 • Green Filé Gumbo 84 • Crock-pot Squirrel and Dumplings 85 • Rabbit Fricassee 86 • Homemade Taso 86 • Hunter's Delight Soup 87 • Meat Sauce Piquant 88 • Frog Legs Sauce Piquant 88 • Sausage Jambalaya 89 • Beef and Cabbage Jambalaya 90 • Creole Spaghetti 90 • Boudin 91 • Chicken and Rice Perlo 92 • Easy Rice Dressing 92 • Bayou Dirty Rice 94 • Baked Rice Dressing 93 • Eggplant Rice Dressing 93 • Bayou Dirty Rice 94 • Chicken Saffron Rice Casserole 95 • Pot-Roasted Duck 96 • Creole Round Steak in Tomatoes 97 • Creamy Chicken and Squash Casserole 97 • Ground Beef Squash Casserole 98 • Zucchini Sausage Casserole 98 • Butterbean Ground Beef Pie 99 • Deep Fried Cajun Chicken or Turkey 99 • Liquid Seasoning 100 • Old-Fashioned Gravy Steaks 100 • Mama's Pork Roast 100 • Fried Alligator 101

Center photo: Brothers Gary and Danny Prejean goofing off after a hunting trip.

Clockwise from left to right: Jon Prejean and daughter Chantelle with their catch. Sisters Shirley Micelli and Lurline Duplechain. Louisiana crab boil. Jim Saizan as a toddler. Canoes at lakeshore. Maque choux or fried corn. My dad, Jim Saizan.

Venison Jerky

My son John created this delicious and easy jerky recipe. A sportsman from a very young age, John has always enjoyed and appreciated wildlife.

4–5	POUNDS VENISON ROAST
1	CUP BROWN SUGAR
1	CUP SOY SAUCE
$1/_2$–1	TEASPOON RED PEPPER
$1/_2$–1	TEASPOON BLACK PEPPER
1	TABLESPOON GROUND GINGER

Slice roast into $1/_4$-inch thick slices. Mix together remaining ingredients to make a marinade. Place venison slices in a bowl and pour marinade on top. Refrigerate for several hours, basting slices hourly. Dry in food dehydrator for $1^1/_2$ days or bake in oven at 200 degrees for 4 hours, turning every 30 minutes or so. Store in an airtight container. Beef can be substituted for venison. Yield: 40–50 slices.

Bacon-Stuffed Venison

My husband, John Corbin, created the next two venison recipes. An avid hunter most of his life, John enjoys cooking and experimenting with different recipes.

1	BACKSTRAP ROAST OR 6–8 1-INCH BACKSTRAP STEAKS
2–3	CUPS BUTTERMILK
5	SLICES BACON
2	GARLIC CLOVES, MINCED
$1/_3$	CUP CARROTS, CHOPPED
2	GARLIC CLOVES, MINCED
$1/_2$	CUP ONION, CHOPPED
$1/_3$	CUP CELERY, CHOPPED
1	CUP MUSHROOMS, SLICED
1	EGG, BEATEN
$1/_2$	CUP PLAIN BREAD CRUMBS
$1/_2$	TEASPOON SALT
$1/_4$	TEASPOON BLACK PEPPER
	ADDITIONAL BACON SLICES

Cut roast in a jelly roll fashion (or butterfly the steaks). Place in a shallow pan and cover with buttermilk. Refrigerate for several hours or overnight. Drain and pat dry. Preheat oven to 325 degrees. In a skillet over medium heat, fry bacon and chopped vegetables until bacon is somewhat crisp and vegetables are soft. Drain. In a bowl, beat the egg. Stir in sautéed vegetables, bread crumbs, and seasonings. Spread this stuffing over the opened roast and roll up jelly-roll fashion. Seal edges with toothpicks. If using steaks, place approximately 2–3 tablespoons of stuffing in each opened steak. Close and wrap the seam with a bacon slice. Seal with toothpicks. Bake roast in about one inch of water in a covered pan for approximately 1 hour and 15 minutes. Baste occasionally. Bake steaks in $1/4$-inch of water, in a covered pan for approximately 40 minutes at 325 degrees. Yield: 6–8 servings.

Venison Sausage

3–4	POUNDS VENISON
$1^1/_2$	POUNDS GROUND PORK
2	TABLESPOONS SALT
$1/_4$	CUP BROWN SUGAR
1	TABLESPOON SAGE
1	TEASPOON RED PEPPER
1	TEASPOON BLACK PEPPER

Cut venison into cube-sized pieces. Mix all ingredients together and grind in a meat grinder or food processor. Shape into small patties approximately $1/_2$-inch thick. Cook in a small amount of oil until brown on both sides (approximately 4–5 minutes). Sausage can be refrigerated for several days or frozen. Yield: 5 pounds.

Venison Marinade

1	STALK GREEN ONION, CHOPPED
$1/_2$	CUP ONION, CHOPPED
1	GARLIC CLOVE, MINCED
$1/_2$	CUP WORCESTERSHIRE SAUCE
4	CUPS WHOLE MILK OR ENOUGH TO COVER MEAT

Combine ingredients. Arrange 2–3 pounds of venison in a shallow container and pour marinade over. Refrigerate for several hours or overnight.

Fried Venison Steaks

Venison Marinade and Fried Venison Steaks come from my younger brother David Saizan.

1	POUND VENISON STEAKS
1	CUP BUTTERMILK
	CAJUN SEASONING (OPTIONAL)
1	CUP ALL-PURPOSE FLOUR
$1/2$	TEASPOON PEPPER
1	TEASPOON SALT
$1/4$	TEASPOON GARLIC POWDER
1	CUP WHOLE MILK
2	EGGS, BEATEN

Soak steaks in buttermilk for several hours or overnight. Drain and pat dry. Sprinkle steaks with Cajun seasoning if desired. In a bowl or plastic bag, combine flour and seasonings. In another bowl, combine beaten eggs and 1 cup milk. Dip steaks in egg, then flour mixture. Cook in one inch of hot vegetable oil for approximately 3–4 minutes. Turn steaks to brown both sides. Yield: 4–6 steaks.

Chicken and Andouille Gumbo

This gumbo recipe was given to me by my brother-in-law Randy Hood. Randy is an Oberlin, Louisiana, native.

$1/3$	CUP OIL
$2/3$	CUP ALL-PURPOSE FLOUR
$1^1/2$	CUPS ONION, CHOPPED
1	CUP GREEN ONION, CHOPPED
5–6	CUPS WATER
1	BAY LEAF
	SALT AND PEPPER TO TASTE
1	CHICKEN CUT IN PIECES
1	POUND ANDOUILLE SAUSAGE, SLICED
6	EGGS, BOILED AND PEELED
	HOT COOKED RICE

Preheat oven to 350 degrees. In a large pot, cook oil and flour over medium heat stirring continuously until lightly browned. Add onion and remove from burner; place in oven and cook for approximately 45 minutes. Stir roux often while in oven. After the roux has turned a dark brown, return to stove and add approximately 5–6 cups of water and remaining ingredients, except for the eggs. Cook for 1 hour. Add the 6 boiled eggs. Cook another 30 minutes. Serve over hot rice with filé and hot sauce. Your favorite sausage can be substituted for the andouille. Yield: 8–12 servings.

The most unique ingredient about this gumbo is the boiled eggs. History suggests that at one time—probably during the depression—eggs replaced meats in the gumbo pot. Andouille sausage is a spicy smoked pork sausage, pronounced **an-doo-ee.** *The gumbo is absolutely delicious.*

Okra Gumbo

$^1/_3$ CUP VEGETABLE OIL

$^2/_3$ CUP ALL-PURPOSE FLOUR

1 CUP ONION, CHOPPED

6 CUPS WATER

1 16-OUNCE BAG FROZEN OKRA, SLICED AND UNBREADED

3 TABLESPOONS PARSLEY FLAKES

1 TABLESPOON RED HOT SAUCE OR TO TASTE

1 LARGE BAY LEAF

SALT AND PEPPER TO TASTE

1 CHICKEN, CUT IN PIECES

1 POUND SMOKED SAUSAGE, SLICED, COOKED, AND DRAINED

HOT COOKED RICE

In a 5-quart pot, cook oil and flour over medium heat, stirring continuously. Add onion when roux is medium brown. Continue cooking until onion are soft. Add water, okra, and seasonings. Bring to a boil. Add meats and bring to a second boil. Reduce heat to medium-low and cover pot. Cook for approximately 45 minutes. Taste and adjust seasonings if necessary. Serve over rice with crackers and filé. Duck can be substituted for the chicken. Yield: 8–12 servings.

Gumbo is African for okra. Having okra and gumbo in the same title is almost redundant. One history source says that gumbo was derived from the French stew bouillabaisse and altered with the meats and vegetables indigenous to Louisiana. Early Louisiana gumbos, I'm told, consisted of guinea fowl, a bird originally from Africa. I have collected several gumbo recipes for this cookbook because I feel it's necessary to show how unique and interesting gumbo can be: from traditional seafood gumbo to chicken and sausage gumbo with boiled eggs. Gumbo, like most Cajun cooking, is up to the cook's imagination!

Green Filé Gumbo

This recipe is contributed by Lurline Duplechain.

1	CUP VEGETABLE OIL
$1/2$	CUP ALL-PURPOSE FLOUR
$1/4$	CUP FILÉ POWDER OR TO TASTE
2	CUPS ONION, CHOPPED
$1/2$	CUP CELERY, CHOPPED
1	CUP BELL PEPPER, CHOPPED
3	CUPS WATER
1	4-OUNCE JAR PIMENTOS
	RED PEPPER FLAKES
1–2	TABLESPOONS KITCHEN BOUQUET FLAVORING FOR COLOR
	SALT AND PEPPER TO TASTE
1	BAY LEAF
1 OR 2	DUCKS, CUT UP
1	POUND SMOKED SAUSAGE, SLICED
2	$10^{1}/_{2}$-OUNCE CANS CHICKEN BROTH
$1/2$	CUP CHOPPED GREEN ONION OR TO TASTE
$1/2$	CUP CHOPPED FRESH PARSLEY OR TO TASTE
	RICE, COOKED

Heat oil in a large gumbo pot on medium heat. Add flour, stirring continuosly until brown. Add filé, stirring for an additional 3 minutes or so. Add onion, celery, and bell pepper. Cook until wilted. Stir in 1 cup water, pimentos, red pepper flakes, Kitchen Bouquet, salt and pepper, and bay leaf (remove bay leaf after 1 hour). Cover and cook for

15 minutes. Add meats, chicken broth, and additional 1–2 cups water to reach the desired stock consistency. Cook for 2 hours or until meats are tender. Stir in green onion and parsley. Serve over rice with crackers. The filé makes the gumbo appear green. The pimento keeps the filé from becoming stringy. Yield: 12–16 servings.

Filé, pronounced fee lay, *was introduced to Louisiana by the Choctaw Indians. My cousin Lurline Duplechain and her husband Coy make their own homemade filé for Green Gumbo. The filé is made by drying sassafras tree leaves until they become brittle, and then grinding them to a coarse powder. They say that old-timers living in lower Cameron Parish on the Gulf contend that if the sassafras leaves are picked during the decrease of the moon in the month of August, the resulting filé will be less stringy when added to the gumbo.*

Crock-pot Squirrel and Dumplings

My good friend Mary Parton contributed this squirrel dumpling recipe. Raised in Chicago, Mary had to quickly learn Cajun cooking after marrying a Louisiana native. Her mother-in-law taught her most of her cooking skills, however with three sons often bringing home "critters" they had caught, Mary had to do her own creative cooking. I'm sure many a Cajun has dined on all sorts of critters from the woods and swamps, including squirrels.

2	SQUIRRELS, CLEANED AND CUT IN PIECES
$1/2$	CUP ONION, CHOPPED
$1/3$	CUP OF CELERY, CHOPPED
$1^1/2$	TEASPOONS CAJUN SEASONING
2	$10^1/2$-OUNCE CANS CREAM OF CHICKEN SOUP
$2^1/2$	CUPS BISCUIT MIX
1	CUP WHOLE MILK

Place squirrel, vegetables, and seasoning in a crock-pot and cover with water. Boil on a medium or low heat overnight. Remove squirrel and debone. Strain broth into a large pot and add enough water to make 9 cups of liquid. Stir in chicken soup and squirrel and bring to a boil. Prepare dumplings by mixing the biscuit mix and milk. Drop by spoonfuls into the boiling mixture. Reduce heat and continue cooking for another 10 minutes. Chicken can be substituted for the squirrel. Yield: 6–8 servings.

Rabbit Fricassee

1	RABBIT, CUT UP
$^1/_4$	CUP PLUS 2 TABLESPOONS ALL-PURPOSE FLOUR
$^3/_4$	TEASPOON SALT OR TO TASTE
$^1/_4$	TEASPOON BLACK PEPPER
$^1/_4$	TEASPOON GARLIC POWDER
$^1/_4$	TEASPOON ONION POWDER
2	TABLESPOONS VEGETABLE OIL
2	CUPS WATER
1	BAY LEAF
1	TABLESPOON DRIED PARSLEY

Mix flour, salt, pepper, and garlic and onion powder. Sprinkle over rabbit pieces. In a skillet over medium heat, brown the rabbit and the remaining 2 tablespoons of flour. Turn rabbit pieces often for even browning. Add the water and remaining spices. Cover and cook over low heat for approximately 1 hour. Serve over rice. Chicken may be substituted for rabbit. Yield: 4–6 servings.

Homemade Taso

Lurline Duplechain contributed the Homemade Taso, Hunter's Delight Soup, and Meat Sauce Piquant recipes.

Cut 4 pounds of meat into $^1/_2$-inch slices. Smoke away from coals for 10–12 hours. Create a marinade of:

$^1/_2$	CUP SALT
$^1/_2$	CUP BROWN SUGAR
1	TEASPOON BLACK PEPPER
1	TEASPOON RED PEPPER
1	TEASPOON CHILI PEPPER

Rub mixture on smoked meats and refrigerate for another 10–12 hours. Taso can be used in almost any recipe requiring meats. Yield: 20–30 servings.

Taso is Cajun spiced meat that has been smoked for several hours and then marinated for another several hours. Pork is the preferred meat, but beef, deer, and turkey can be used also.

Hunter's Delight Soup

1	16-OUNCE BAG PINTO BEANS
3	POUNDS CUBED BEEF, PORK, OR VENISON
1	POUND GROUND CHUCK
	SALT AND PEPPER TO TASTE
2–3	TABLESPOONS COOKING OIL
2	CUPS ONION, CHOPPED
2	GARLIC CLOVES, CHOPPED
2	10-OUNCE CANS TOMATOES WITH CHILI PEPPERS
1	6-OUNCE CAN TOMATO PASTE
1	8-OUNCE CAN TOMATO SAUCE
$1/4$	CUP CHILI POWDER
1	TEASPOON OREGANO
1	TEASPOON CUMIN
$1/2$	TEASPOON GARLIC POWDER
1	TEASPOON CAJUN SEASONING OR TO TASTE

Cook bag of dry pintos according to directions. Set aside. Salt and pepper the meats. In a large pot, cover bottom with cooking oil and heat on medium. Cook meats until browned. Add onion, garlic, and tomatoes, cooking until tender. Add tomato paste and sauce and the remaining seasonings. Cook on low for an hour, stirring occasionally. Water may be added to thin the soup. Taste and season again if necessary. Serve soup over pinto beans with tortillas. Yield: 15–20 servings.

Meat Sauce Piquant

2–3	TABLESPOONS COOKING OIL
1	POUND BONELESS BEEF STEW MEAT
1	POUND BONELESS PORK, CUBED
1	POUND BONELESS CHICKEN, CUBED
$1/2$	POUND TASO (SEE P. 86)
$1/2$	POUND SMOKED SAUSAGE, SLICED
1	10-OUNCE CAN TOMATOES WITH CHILI PEPPERS
1	15-OUNCE CAN STEWED TOMATOES
1	10-OUNCE CAN BEEF GRAVY
1	8-OUNCE CAN TOMATO SAUCE
1	4-OUNCE CAN MUSHROOMS, DRAINED
3	CUPS ONION, CHOPPED
1	CUP BELL PEPPER, CHOPPED
1	BUNCH GREEN ONION, CHOPPED
1	GARLIC CLOVE, MINCED
2	TABLESPOONS DRIED PARSLEY FLAKES
	SALT AND PEPPER TO TASTE
	HOT COOKED RICE

Coat the bottom of a large stock pot with cooking oil. Add meats and cook until half done. Add all other ingredients and enough water to thin the sauce. Simmer for 2–3 hours. Serve over rice. Yield: 18–22 servings.

Frog Legs Sauce Piquant

1	DOZEN FROG LEGS
1	TEASPOON SALT, DIVIDED
$1/2$	TEASPOON RED PEPPER
$1/4$	TEASPOON GARLIC POWDER
$1/4$	CUP VEGETABLE OIL
$1/4$	CUP ALL-PURPOSE FLOUR
$1/4$	CUP BELL PEPPER, CHOPPED
$1/4$	CUP CELERY, CHOPPED
$1/4$	CUP GREEN ONION, CHOPPED
2	TABLESPOONS DRIED PARSLEY FLAKES
1	15-OUNCE CAN STEWED TOMATOES

Rinse and dry frog legs. Season with half the salt and all of the red pepper and garlic powder. Fry in hot oil, turning often until golden brown. Remove and drain. To the remaining oil, add flour until it reaches the consistency of a thin paste. Cook on medium heat to a medium brown, stirring continuously. To the browned roux, add the onion, bell pepper, and celery. Cook until soft, approximately 5 minutes. Add the remaining ingredients including frog legs. Bring to a boil and reduce heat, simmering for an additional 15 minutes. Serve over rice. Chicken pieces can be substituted for the frog legs. Yield: 6–8 servings.

Sausage Jambalaya

1	POUND SMOKED SAUSAGE, SLICED
1	TABLESPOON VEGETABLE OIL
1	TABLESPOON ALL-PURPOSE FLOUR OR PREPARED ROUX
$1/2$	CUP ONION, CHOPPED
$1/4$	CUP CELERY, CHOPPED
$1/4$	CUP BELL PEPPER, CHOPPED
$1/4$	CUP GREEN ONION, CHOPPED
2	CUPS WATER
1	CUP RICE, UNCOOKED
$1/4$	CUP DRIED PARSLEY FLAKES
1	TEASPOON SALT
$1/2$	TEASPOON RED HOT SAUCE
$1/4$	TEASPOON BLACK PEPPER
	DASH OF GARLIC POWDER

Slice sausage into $1/4$-inch slices. Place in a large skillet and cover with water. Boil sausage over medium heat until water has evaporated. Repeat process another time until sausage starts to brown. Add vegetable oil and chopped vegetables to skillet. Sprinkle flour on top and continue cooking until the flour begins to brown. Add water, rice, and seasonings. Cover and cook over low heat for approximately 30 minutes or until water is absorbed. One tablespoon of prepared roux may be substituted for the flour. See page 51 for a prepared roux recipe. Yield: 4–6 servings.

Beef and Cabbage Jambalaya

1	POUND GROUND CHUCK
1	CUP ONION, CHOPPED
$1/2$	CUP CELERY, CHOPPED
$1/4$	CUP BELL PEPPER, CHOPPED
1	SMALL HEAD CABBAGE, CHOPPED
1	10-OUNCE CAN TOMATOES WITH CHILI PEPPERS
1	CUP RICE, UNCOOKED
2	CUPS WATER
$1/4$	TEASPOON GARLIC POWDER
	SALT AND BLACK PEPPER TO TASTE

In a large skillet over medium heat, cook ground chuck, onion, celery, and bell pepper until the meat is browned and the vegetables are soft. Drain off grease. Add remaining ingredients. Cover and simmer for approximately 30 minutes or until the rice and cabbage are cooked. Yield: 6–8 servings.

Creole Spaghetti

This very unique recipe is contributed by Lurline Duplechain.

1	16-OUNCE PACKAGE SPAGHETTI
1	POUND GROUND BEEF
$1^1/2$	CUPS ONION, CHOPPED
1	CLOVE GARLIC
$1/2$	CUP BELL PEPPER, CHOPPED
1	$15^1/2$-OUNCE CAN CREAM CORN
1	$10^1/2$-OUNCE CAN TOMATO SOUP
1	4-OUNCE CAN MUSHROOMS, DRAINED
1	TEASPOON WORCESTERSHIRE SAUCE
2	TEASPOONS CAJUN SEASONING OR TO TASTE
1	CUP CHEDDAR CHEESE, GRATED

Cook spaghetti according to directions. Drain and set aside. Preheat oven to 350 degrees. In a large skillet over medium heat, cook the ground beef, onion, garlic, and bell pepper. Drain off any excess oil. Add remaining ingredients except spaghetti and cheese. Stir well. Stir in spaghetti and pour into a casserole dish. Top with grated cheese. Bake until bubbly, approximately 20 minutes. Yield: 8–10 servings.

Boudin

3	3-FOOT SAUSAGE CASINGS
2	POUNDS GROUND PORK
$1/2$	POUND GROUND CHICKEN LIVERS
3	CUPS ONION, CHOPPED
1	BAY LEAF, CRUMBLED
5	WHOLE BLACK PEPPERCORNS
4	TEASPOONS SALT
1	CUP PARSLEY, CHOPPED
1	BUNCH GREEN ONION, CHOPPED
3–4	GARLIC CLOVES, CHOPPED
5	CUPS WHITE RICE, COOKED
1	TEASPOON SAGE
$2^1/2$	TEASPOONS RED PEPPER
1	TEASPOON BLACK PEPPER

Soak casings in warm water until pliable (2–3 hours). In a skillet over medium heat, brown pork, liver, and onion. Drain. Add water to skillet, just covering meats. Add bay leaf and peppercorns. Cover and boil for 1 hour. Drain; discard peppercorns. Grind meats in a food processor or meat grinder. Transfer to a large bowl and add the remaining ingredients, mixing well. Taste and make any necessary adjustments. After the casings have been rinsed inside and out, knot one end. Spoon mixture into casings until filled. Tie a knot at the other end. To cook, prick holes throughout the sausage and place in a pot of hot water. Boil gently for approximately 30 minutes. Boudin may be reheated in the microwave on medium heat, or browned in a small amount of oil. It can be frozen or refrigerated up to 1 week. Yield: 7 or 8 12-inch sausages.

Recipe Variation: Boudin Balls—Follow directions for boudin, but omit casings. Scoop up spoonfuls and shape into balls. Roll in seasoned bread crumbs and fry in hot oil until golden brown. Yield: 75–100 balls, depending on size.

Boudin, pronounced boo da, *is French for blood meat. It is a delicious, spicy rice and pork stuffed sausage, similar to the French sausage* boudin noir. *No doubt the French settlers tried to duplicate the French sausage they remembered, however they added rice which was plentiful in Louisiana and other parts of the South.*

Chicken and Rice Perlo is a very old dish my great-grandmother from northern Florida use to make. During my research, I ran across two spellings and pronunciations of this recipe. I've heard it pronounced per-loo. And it's sometimes spelled perleau. This recipe is now in its fifth known generation—it may even precede my great-grandmother's generation.

Chicken and Rice Perlo

1	3-POUND CHICKEN, CUT IN PIECES
1	MEDIUM ONION, QUARTERED
$1/2$	CUP CELERY, CHOPPED
3	CUPS RICE, UNCOOKED
	SALT AND PEPPER TO TASTE

Place chicken pieces and vegetables in a 5 or 6 quart pot. Cover with water and season with salt and pepper to taste. Boil for 1 to 1 $1/2$ hours or until tender. Strain liquid and save, discarding celery and onion. Skin and debone chicken and cut into bite size pieces. In the empty pot, combine 3 cups of rice, 6 cups of the chicken broth (add water if there aren't quite 6 cups of broth), and the boneless chicken. Cook over low to medium heat for 25 minutes or until rice has absorbed the liquid. Yield: 8–10 servings.

Easy Rice Dressing

1	POUND GROUND BEEF
$1/4$	CUP MARGARINE OR BUTTER
$1/3$	CUP BELL PEPPER, CHOPPED
$1/3$	CUP ONION, CHOPPED
$1/3$	CUP CELERY, CHOPPED
$1/3$	CUP GREEN ONION, CHOPPED
1	TABLESPOON ALL-PURPOSE FLOUR OR PREPARED ROUX
$1/2$	TEASPOON CAJUN SEASONING
2	CUBES BEEF BOUILLON
1	TEASPOON RED HOT SAUCE
1	CUP RICE, UNCOOKED

In a skillet over medium heat, cook and drain ground beef. Add margarine or butter and vegetables and cook until tender. Add flour and cook until flour begins to brown. Add remaining ingredients and cook covered for 25 minutes or until rice is tender. Yield: 5–7 servings.

Baked Rice Dressing

1	POUND GROUND BEEF, UNCOOKED
$1/2$	CUP GREEN ONION, CHOPPED
$1/2$	CUP CELERY, CHOPPED
$1/4$	TEASPOON BELL PEPPER, CHOPPED
1	$10^1/_2$-OUNCE CAN ONION SOUP
1	$10^1/_2$-OUNCE CAN CREAM OF CHICKEN SOUP
$1/2$	TEASPOON RED PEPPER
$1/4$	TEASPOON BLACK PEPPER
$1/4$	TEASPOON GARLIC POWDER
1	TEASPOON SALT
1	CUP RICE, UNCOOKED
1	TEASPOON KITCHEN BOUQUET FLAVORING

Preheat oven to 350 degrees. Mix all ingredients in a casserole dish. Bake covered for $1^1/_2$ hours. Cajun seasoning can be substituted for the seasonings. Yield: 5–7 servings.

Eggplant Rice Dressing

Follow directions above for Easy Rice Dressing. Before serving, stir in one eggplant that has been peeled, boiled, and mashed. Heat through before serving. Squash can be substituted for eggplant. Yield: 6–8 servings.

Bayou Dirty Rice

1	POUND CHICKEN LIVERS
1	POUND CHICKEN GIZZARDS
6–8	BONELESS PORK CHOPS
$1/2$	POUND GROUND BEEF
3	TABLESPOONS OIL
1	CUP WATER
$1^1/_2$	CUPS ONION, CHOPPED
$1/2$	CUP PARSLEY, CHOPPED
1	CUP CELERY, CHOPPED
1	CUP GREEN ONION, CHOPPED
3	CUPS RICE, COOKED AND HOT
	SALT AND PEPPER TO TASTE

While chicken livers are frozen, slice into thin pieces with a sharp knife. Set aside to thaw. Grind or finely chop gizzards and pork chops. Brown gizzards, pork chops, and ground beef in oil. Stir in 1 cup water and cook an additional 10 minutes. Add vegetables and cook over medium heat until tender, adding more water if needed. Stir in the cooked rice and thawed liver; cook until the liver is done. Season to taste. Yield: 12–15 servings.

Dirty Rice versus Rice Dressing. The differences: dirty rice is a rice dish made with livers and giblets. These not only give the dish a "dirty" appearance but a wild taste as well. Rice dressing is an easier and quicker version of dirty rice without the livers and giblets. Both are delicious and excellent served as side dishes or used as stuffing for chicken, turkey, or geese.

Saffron is a pungent, deep orange spice made from the dried stigmas of a purple-flowered crocus. It has been used in medicine and to flavor and color foods.

Chicken Saffron Rice Casserole

This delicious Chicken Saffron Rice Casserole was contributed by Shirley Rodrigue Micelli. A Lake Charles, Louisiana, native, Shirley has worked many years for a well-known weight management company and enjoys good food and cooking healthier Cajun foods.

2	5-OZ. PACKAGES YELLOW SAFFRON RICE MIX
1	CUP ONION, CHOPPED
1	CUP BELL PEPPER, CHOPPED
1	CUP EGGPLANT, DICED
1	CUP MUSHROOMS, SLICED
$^1/_2$	CUP MARGARINE OR BUTTER
1	10-OUNCE CAN TOMATOES WITH CHILI PEPPERS
1	$10^1/_2$-OUNCE CAN CREAM OF MUSHROOM SOUP
1	$10^1/_2$-OUNCE CAN CREAM OF BROCCOLI CHEESE SOUP
2	CUPS CHICKEN, COOKED AND CUBED
1	CUP CHEDDAR CHEESE, GRATED

Preheat oven to 350 degrees. Cook rice according to directions. Meanwhile, in a skillet over medium-low heat, sauté vegetables in melted margarine or butter until tender. Add canned tomatoes and heat through. Remove from heat and stir in remaining ingredients except the rice. Spread rice in a greased casserole dish and pour the chicken mixture over. Sprinkle with cheese if desired. Bake for approximately 35–40 minutes. Cool slightly before serving. Yield: 8–12 servings.

Pot-Roasted Duck

My cousin Danny Prejean contributed this Pot-Roasted Duck recipe from his father's collection. Danny says that when his grandmother cooked this dish, she referred to it as "burning the ducks." Danny comes from a family of five boys; they were always bringing something interesting home to be cooked!

2–3	DUCKS
	CAJUN SEASONING TO TASTE
	WHOLE GARLIC CLOVES TO TASTE
1	POUND BACON
$^1/_2$	POUND SMOKED PORK OR BEEF SAUSAGE, SLICED
1	BLACK IRON POT WITH LID
	"FREE TIME"
	HOT COOKED RICE

Prepare ducks and season with cajun seasoning. With a knife, make a slit in each duck's breast and insert garlic cloves inside. Set ducks aside. On medium heat, cook the bacon in the iron pot until cooked but not crisp. Remove bacon. Place the ducks in the hot bacon grease and cook until brown. Continue turning ducks so they will not burn. After the ducks have been browned, add approximately 2 inches of water to the pot. Add the sausage and bacon and cover. Continue cooking on medium-low heat for approximately 4–5 hours or until the meat starts to fall off the bones. As the water cooks down, continue to add water so that the pot always has a few inches of water. Towards the end, the water will turn into nice browned gravy. Serve over rice. For small ducks, cook 3–4 hours; medium ducks, 4–5 hours; and geese, 5–6 hours. If using wild ducks, soak overnight in water and one cup cider vinegar to remove the "mud" taste. Yield: 4–6 servings.

Creole Round Steak in Tomatoes

According to my great-aunt Doris, her mother Eva Rodrigue often made this Creole dish for breakfast. The spicy peppers were from her Portuguese and Spanish side; she no doubt had a strong stomach to handle something so spicy so early in the morning.

$1^1/_2$	POUNDS ROUND STEAKS
$^1/_4$	CUP ALL-PURPOSE FLOUR
	SALT AND PEPPER TO TASTE
2	TABLESPOONS OIL
$^1/_2$	CUP CELERY, CHOPPED
$^1/_4$	CUP ONION, CHOPPED
1 OR 2	HOT PEPPERS, CHOPPED (OPTIONAL)
1	16-OUNCE CAN TOMATOES
1	TEASPOON WORCESTERSHIRE SAUCE
$^1/_2$	CUP WATER

Cut the steaks into serving portions. Sprinkle with salt and pepper. Dredge in the flour. In a skillet, heat the oil and brown the meat. Reduce heat and add chopped vegetables. Sauté until soft. Add remaining ingredients and $^1/_2$ cup water. Cover skillet and simmer for 1 $^1/_2$ to 2 hours. Serve over rice if desired. Yield: 6–8 servings.

Creamy Chicken and Squash Casserole

$1^1/_2$	POUNDS FRESH SUMMER SQUASH, PEELED AND CUBED
$1^1/_2$	CUPS ONION, CHOPPED
1	$10^1/_2$-OUNCE CAN CREAM OF CHICKEN SOUP
1	8-OUNCE CARTON SOUR CREAM
2	CUPS CHICKEN, COOKED AND CUBED
$^1/_2$	CUP MARGARINE OR BUTTER
1	8-OUNCE PACKAGED HERBED STUFFING MIX

Preheat oven to 350 degrees. Boil squash and onion in salted water. Drain. Add soup, sour cream, and cooked chicken. Set aside. Combine melted margarine or butter and stuffing mix. Spread half in casserole dish. Pour squash mixture on top. Spread remaining stuffing mixture over that. Bake for 30 minutes. Yields: 6–8 servings.

Ground Beef Squash Casserole

My cousin Susan Thibodeaux Betancourt of Baton Rouge contributed this delicious Ground Beef Squash Casserole. This recipe is very simple to make.

3	CUPS FRESH SUMMER SQUASH, PEELED AND CUBED
$3/4$	CUP ONION, CHOPPED
1	5-OUNCE CAN EVAPORATED MILK
2	CUPS PLAIN BREAD CRUMBS
1	TEASPOON SALT
$1/2$	TEASPOON RED PEPPER
2	EGGS, BEATEN
6	TABLESPOONS MARGARINE OR BUTTER, MELTED
1	POUND GROUND BEEF, BROWNED
1	CUP CHEDDAR CHEESE, GRATED AND DIVIDED

Preheat oven to 350 degrees. Cook squash and onion in a small amount of water until tender. Drain and pour into a greased casserole dish with half the cheese and the remaining ingredients. Mix well. Bake for 30 minutes covered. Uncover and sprinkle remaining cheese on top. Bake for an additional 10 minutes or until cheese melts. Yields: 6–8 servings.

Zucchini Sausage Casserole

$1/2$	POUND BREAKFAST SAUSAGE
$1/2$	CUP ONION, CHOPPED
4 OR 5	LARGE ZUCCHINIS, PEELED AND CUBED
2	EGGS, BEATEN
$1/2$	CUP PARMESAN CHEESE
$1/2$	CUP CHEDDAR CHEESE, GRATED
1	CUP BUTTER CRACKERS, CRUSHED
	RED AND BLACK PEPPER TO TASTE

Preheat oven to 350 degrees. In a skillet over medium heat, cook the sausage and onion. Drain and set aside. Meanwhile, boil the zucchinis in a small amount of salted water until tender. Drain and mash. Pour all ingredients except cracker crumbs into a casserole dish. Sprinkle with cracker crumbs. Bake for approximately 30 to 40 minutes or until golden brown. Yield: 4–6 servings.

Butterbean Ground Beef Pie

Billie Corbin of Jasper, Alabama, contributed this recipe and says the original dates back to the 1930s. Billie enjoys cooking and collecting unique recipes such as this one.

1	POUND GROUND BEEF
1¹/₂	CUPS BELL PEPPER, CHOPPED
1	CUP ONION, CHOPPED
2	CUPS BUTTERBEANS, COOKED **OR**
1	15-OUNCE CAN GREEN LIMA BEANS
2	15-OUNCE CANS NIBBLETS CORN, DRAINED
2	10-OUNCE CANS TOMATOES WITH CHILI PEPPERS
1	CUP CHEDDAR CHEESE, GRATED
1	6 1/2-OUNCE PACKAGE CORNBREAD MIX

Preheat oven to 350 degrees. In a skillet over medium heat, cook ground beef, bell pepper, and onion. Drain. In a casserole dish, layer ingredients as follows: butter beans, ground beef mixture, corn, tomatoes, cheese, and finally the dry cornbread mix. Bake for 30 minutes or until brown. Yield: 6–8 servings.

Cornbread has been made for hundreds of years; cornbread mixes were introduced around the 1930s. No doubt this recipe has been modernized somewhat since the original version.

Deep Fried Cajun Chicken or Turkey

1	WHOLE CHICKEN OR TURKEY
	SEASONING INJECTOR
	LIQUID SEASONING MIXTURE (SEE P. 100)
	PEANUT OIL, ENOUGH TO COVER BIRD
	CAJUN SEASONING

Inject liquid seasoning liberally into the chicken or turkey. Sprinkle bird liberally with Cajun seasoning. Let sit for 30 minutes. Preheat oil to 350 degrees in the turkey fryer. Carefully lower bird into hot oil. For each pound, cook 9–11 minutes.

Liquid Seasoning

1¹/₂	CUPS WATER
¹/₄	CUP MARGARINE OR BUTTER, MELTED
1	TABLESPOON SMOKE-FLAVORED LIQUID SEASONING
2	TABLESPOONS CAJUN SEASONING
1	TABLESPOON LEMON JUICE

Heat ingredients in a saucepan. Taste and adjust seasonings if desired. Store in an airtight container and refrigerate. Reheat when ready to use. Yield: 2 cups.

Old-Fashioned Gravy Steaks

2	POUNDS CHUCK STEAK, FAT REMOVED
	SALT AND PEPPER TO TASTE
1	CUP ALL-PURPOSE FLOUR
	VEGETABLE OIL FOR FRYING
3–4	TABLESPOONS ADDITIONAL ALL-PURPOSE FLOUR FOR GRAVY
1	ONION, CHOPPED
2	CUPS WATER

Cut steak into serving pieces. Season with salt and pepper. Dredge steaks in flour and pan fry in one-inch deep hot oil. After browning both sides, remove and drain. Pour off all but 3 tablespoons of oil from frying pan. Leave any pan drippings and add 3–4 tablespoons of flour. Brown the flour and add the chopped onion. Reduce heat and continue cooking onion until soft. Add 2 cups of water and bring gravy to a boil. Put steaks back in the gravy, cover, and cook for one hour. Check occasionally to see if more water is needed. Serve over rice or mashed potatoes. Yield: 8–10 servings.

Mama's Pork Roast

1	3 ¹/₂ TO 4 POUND BOSTON BUTT PORK ROAST
	SALT AND PEPPER TO TASTE
2–3	GARLIC CLOVES
1	TABLESPOON VEGETABLE OIL
	WATER FOR GRAVY
4¹/₂	CUPS ONION, CHOPPED
1	TABLESPOON CORNSTARCH
	HOT COOKED RICE

Season roast with salt and pepper. Stuff garlic cloves into roast with a knife. In a heavy roaster on medium heat, brown roast in about 1 tablespoon of vegetable oil. Add $^1/_2$ cup water and onion. Cook until onion begin to brown slightly. Continue to cook roast and onion, by adding small amounts of water when needed to prevent burning. This continual process takes about 1 hour. Next add about 1 $^1/_2$ cups of water. Continue cooking the roast for another hour. Just before the roast is done, add 1 tablespoon cornstarch mixed with a little water to thicken the gravy. Serve with cooked rice. Yield: 8–10 servings.

Fried Alligator

This unique recipe is provided by my cousin Lurline Duplechain.

2	POUNDS ALLIGATOR MEAT
1	4-OUNCE JAR MUSTARD
1	16-OUNCE BOTTLE ITALIAN DRESSING
$^1/_2$	CUP LEMON JUICE
1	LARGE ONION, SLICED
	SALT TO TASTE
	RED AND BLACK PEPPER TO TASTE
	ALL-PURPOSE FLOUR AND OIL FOR FRYING

Cut alligator meat into 1-inch pieces. Combine the remaining ingredients in a bowl. Soak the meat in this marinade overnight. The next day, drain off the marinade. Drop gator pieces into a plastic bag with flour. Coat well. In a skillet, deep fry to a golden brown as you would chicken. Yield: 30–40 pieces.

Alligators are indigenous to the Gulf coastal swamps and are considered a delicacy. I was very surprised to hear that a nationwide grocery store chain carries gator meat from time to time, according to my son-in-law Jeff Burleson who is a meat department manager at a Tennessee store. According to Jeff, the gator meat is ordered mainly during the week of the University of Florida vs. University of Tennessee football game. So for gator meat you just have to ask your grocery store meat manager.

Candies, Cookies, & Bars

CANDIES

Holiday Balls 104 • Holiday Date Roll 105 • Fruit Balls 105 • Creole Pralines 106 • Chocolate Pralines 106 • Blonde Microwave Pralines 106 • Praline Pecans 107 • Favorite Fudge 107 • Microwave Nut Brittle 108 • Walnut Bourbon Balls 109 • Syrup Taffy 109

COOKIES & BARS

Nutty Coconut Bars 110 • Date Nut Bars 110 • Praline Pecan Chews 111 • Praline Frosting 111 • Pecan Crunchies 112 • Pecan Puffs 112 • Snowballs 113 • Praline Snowballs 113 • Pecan Pie Bars 114 • Lemon Praline Drops 114 • Upside-down Chocolate Chip Praline Brownies 115

Center photo: Alvinette Prejean, approximately five years old, poses for a picture dressed as Santa Claus.

Clockwise from left to right: Boats in harbor. Robertha Rodrigue Saizan and Charlotte Saizan pose with their holiday pies. My first birthday cake—a triple-layer! John and Caleb Corbin. My fourth birthday party in Louisiana. Ralph Prejean. Shirley Micelli stops for a picture at the Rodrigue family reunion.

Candy Techniques

Thread Stage—230–233 degrees
  When a teaspoon is dipped into the hot mixture and removed, the candy falls off the spoon in a fine, thin thread.
Soft-Ball Stage—234–240 degrees
  When a ball of candy is removed from a cold water test, the candy quickly loses its shape and runs between your fingers.
Firm-Ball Stage—244–248 degrees
  When a ball of candy is removed from a cold water test, it holds its shape, but flattens at room temperature.
Hard-Ball Stage—250–266 degrees
  When a ball of candy is removed from a cold water test, it holds its shape until being pressed.
Soft-Crack Stage—270–290 degrees
  When dropped into water, thin, elastic, but pliable threads form.
Hard-Crack Stage—295–310 degrees
  When dropped into water, hard, brittle threads form that easily break.

Holiday Balls

1   14-OUNCE CAN SWEETENED CONDENSED MILK
2   16-OUNCE BOXES CONFECTIONER'S SUGAR
$^1/_2$ CUP MARGARINE OR BUTTER
1   7-OUNCE PACKAGE FLAKED COCONUT
2   TEASPOONS VANILLA
2   CUPS PECAN PIECES
1   12-OUNCE BAG CHOCOLATE CHIPS, ANY FLAVOR
1   SMALL CUBE PARAFFIN WAX

In a mixing bowl, combine first six ingredients, mixing well. Roll into balls and freeze overnight. The next day, melt chocolate chips with a cube of paraffin wax. With toothpicks, dip the balls into the chocolate mixture. Place on wax paper to dry. Yield: 2–3 dozen.

Holiday Date Rolls are a traditional Christmas candy. Doris Rodrigue Hancock made this candy every year for her very large family. She has eight children, seventeen grandchildren, fifty-two great-grandchildren, and three on the way at last count. She said she decided to stop making the date roll when the family got too large. Another traditional Christmas candy is Fruit Balls, contributed by Lurline Rodrigue Duplechain and Holiday Balls, contributed by Nell Williams Corbin.

Holiday Date Roll

2   CUPS GRANULATED SUGAR
1   CUP WHOLE MILK
1   10-OUNCE PACKAGE DATES, CHOPPED
1   TABLESPOON MARGARINE OR BUTTER
1   CUP PECANS, CHOPPED
     PINCH OF SALT
1   TEASPOON VANILLA

Bring sugar and milk to a hard boil. Add remaining ingredients except vanilla. Stir continuously until a semi-firm soft ball stage. Remove from heat and stir in vanilla. When candy is cool enough to handle, shape into a log and wrap in a damp cloth. Chill until firm and ready to slice. Store refrigerated in an airtight container. Yield: 4 pounds.

Fruit Balls

1   POUND FIGS, DRY
1   POUND RAISINS
1   POUND DATES, PITTED
2   POUNDS PECANS, SHELLED
1   CUP CITRUS JUICE
     CONFECTIONER'S SUGAR

Grind fruits and pecans. Soak in fruit juice and refrigerate for one week. Roll into balls and dip into confectioner's sugar. Orange juice and lemon juice are great in this recipe! Yield: 3–4 dozen.

Pralines are said to have been invented in the 1600s by a Frenchman's cook. No doubt Frenchman Jean-Baptiste Bienville had a stash of these when he came to New Orleans as colonial governor.

Creole Pralines

This recipe is a favorite of Jerry and Joyce Rodrigue.

2	CUPS GRANULATED SUGAR
1	CUP BROWN SUGAR
$1/2$	CUP BUTTER
1	CUP WHOLE MILK
2	TABLESPOONS DARK CORN SYRUP
3	CUPS PECAN HALVES

Combine all ingredients except pecans into a 3-quart saucepan and cook for 20 minutes on medium heat. Add the pecans after the mixture begins to boil. Continue cooking until the syrup reaches a soft-ball stage. Remove from heat and mix well. Drop by teaspoons onto wax paper. Cool before removing. Yield: 36–40 pieces.

Chocolate Pralines

Follow directions above. After removing from heat, stir in 1 cup chocolate chips. Mix well and drop by teaspoons onto wax paper. Cool before removing.

Blonde Microwave Pralines

2	CUPS GRANULATED SUGAR
$1/2$	CUP WHOLE MILK
$1/2$	CUP LIGHT CORN SYRUP
2	TABLESPOONS MARGARINE OR BUTTER
1	TABLESPOON VANILLA
2	CUPS PECAN HALVES

In a large microwave safe bowl, combine all ingredients except vanilla and pecans. Microwave on high for 5 minutes. Stir and turn bowl. Microwave another 8 minutes, stirring and checking candy stage halfway through. Remove and beat vigorously or until color dulls, about 4 or 5 minutes or until a soft-ball stage is reached. Stir in vanilla and pecans, and drop by spoonfuls onto wax paper. For the traditional colored praline, add vanilla in the beginning with the other ingredients. Microwaves, like most conventional ovens, cook differently. Using a candy thermometer or water test is very important in microwave candy cooking. Yield: 28–32 pieces.

Praline Pecans

$1^1/_2$ CUPS PECAN HALVES
$^1/_2$ CUP BROWN SUGAR
2   TABLESPOONS MARGARINE OR BUTTER
1   TEASPOON DARK CORN SYRUP
$^1/_2$ TEASPOON VANILLA

In a saucepan, combine all ingredients. Cook until mixture comes to a boil and pecans are well coated. Spread on a greased cookie sheet to cool. Store in an airtight container. Yield: $1^1/_2$ cups.

Favorite Fudge

2   CUPS GRANULATED SUGAR
$^3/_4$ CUP EVAPORATED MILK
16   LARGE MARSHMALLOWS OR 1 CUP CREME
$^1/_4$ CUP MARGARINE OR BUTTER
$^1/_4$ TEASPOON SALT
6   OUNCES CHOCOLATE CHIPS, ANY FLAVOR
1   CUP PECAN PIECES
1   TABLESPOON VANILLA

Combine sugar, milk, marshmallows, margarine or butter, and salt in a heavy saucepan. Cook over medium heat, stirring constantly. Bring mixture to a boil and continue boiling for 5 minutes. Remove from heat and stir in remaining ingredients. Spread in a buttered pan. Cool and cut into squares. Yield: 3 pounds or 16–20 pieces.

One of the earliest of the candy brittles was made with benne seeds or sesame seeds. African slaves introduced sesame seeds to New Orleans. Benne brittle is very similar to our modern-day nut brittles.

Microwave Nut Brittle

This microwave nut brittle is absolutely perfect. However, raw nuts work best, and microwave cooking time does vary slightly from oven to oven.

1	CUP PECAN PIECES
1	CUP GRANULATED SUGAR
$1/2$	CUP LIGHT CORN SYRUP
$1/8$	TEASPOON SALT
1	TEASPOON MARGARINE OR BUTTER
1	TEASPOON VANILLA
1	TEASPOON BAKING SODA

In a microwave-safe bowl, mix pecans, sugar, corn syrup, and salt. Cook on high for 4 minutes. Stir and turn bowl. Cook on high for another 4 minutes. Add margarine or butter and vanilla, stirring well. Cook on high for 1 more minute. Stir in baking soda and pour onto a buttered cookie sheet. When cool, break into pieces. Other nuts can be used in place of pecans. Microwaves, like most conventional ovens cook differently. You may need to alter the cooking time slightly. Yield: 1 pound.

Walnut Bourbon Balls

1/4   CUP COCOA, SIFTED
1   CUP CONFECTIONERS' SUGAR, SIFTED
1/4   CUP BOURBON
3   TABLESPOONS DARK CORN SYRUP
2   CUPS VANILLA WAFER CRUMBS
1   CUP WALNUTS, CHOPPED
       ADDITIONAL CONFECTIONER'S SUGAR

In a bowl, sift together cocoa and confectioner's sugar. Stir in bourbon and corn syrup. Add vanilla wafers and pecans, mixing well. Shape into 1-inch balls and roll in additional sugar. Orange juice can be substituted for the bourbon. Yield: 24 to 36 balls.

Syrup Taffy

2   CUPS GRANULATED SUGAR
1   CUP CANE SYRUP
1/3   CUP WATER
2   TEASPOONS WHITE DISTILLED VINEGAR
2   TABLESPOONS MARGARINE OR BUTTER
1/2   TEASPOON BAKING SODA
       EXTRA MARGARINE OR BUTTER

Butter the sides of a large, heavy saucepan. Add sugar, syrup, and water. Over medium heat, stir constantly until mixture begins to boil. Stir in vinegar and continue to cook until the hard-ball stage is reached. Remove from heat and stir in the margarine or butter and baking soda. Pour into a large buttered pan. Cool until the taffy is easy to handle. With buttered hands, pull until the taffy becomes gold in color. Divide taffy into fourths and shape each into 1/2-inch strands. With scissors cut each strand into bite sized pieces. Wrap in wax paper. Molasses or corn syrup can be substituted for the cane syrup. Yield: 1 1/2 pounds.

Nutty Coconut Bars

1¹/₂   CUPS BROWN SUGAR, DIVIDED
¹/₂   CUP MARGARINE OR BUTTER, MELTED
1   CUP ALL-PURPOSE FLOUR
¹/₄   TEASPOON SALT
2   EGGS, BEATEN
1   TEASPOON VANILLA
1   CUP FLAKED COCONUT
1   CUP WALNUTS, CHOPPED

CRUST:
Preheat oven to 350 degrees. In a bowl, combine $1/2$ cup of brown sugar and margarine or butter until well blended. Stir in flour. Press dough into an 8x8-inch baking pan. Bake for 10 minutes.

FILLING:
Combine remaining 1 cup brown sugar, salt, beaten eggs, vanilla, coconut, and nuts. Mix well. Pour over baked crust. Bake an additional 25–30 minutes at 350 degrees. Cool and cut into bars. Yield: 9–12 bars.

Date Nut Bars

Lurline Rodrigue Duplechain contributed this date bar recipe. This delicious candy-like bar is wonderful at Christmas.

1   CUP GRANULATED SUGAR
1   CUP ALL-PURPOSE FLOUR
1   TEASPOON BAKING POWDER
¹/₂   TEASPOON SALT
3   EGGS
1   TEASPOON VANILLA
1   TABLESPOON WHOLE MILK
1   POUND DATES, CHOPPED
¹/₂   CUP NUTS, CHOPPED
    CONFECTIONER'S SUGAR

Preheat oven to 325 degrees. Sift dry ingredients together. Set aside. In another bowl, beat eggs and vanilla. Stir in dry ingredients. Add the milk, dates, and nuts, mixing well. Spread dough in a greased and floured 9x13 baking pan. Bake for 30–35 minutes. Cool and cut into strips. Roll in confectioner's sugar if desired. Yield: 16–20 bars.

Praline Pecan Chews

I have found this bar cookie recipe, similar to a blonde brownie, to have many names. I have also run across a delicious praline frosting that compliments the bars very well. Together they are yummy!

$1/2$	CUP MARGARINE OR BUTTER
1	16-OUNCE BOX BROWN SUGAR
2	EGGS
2	CUPS BISCUIT MIX
1	TEASPOON VANILLA
1	CUP PECANS, CHOPPED

Preheat oven to 350 degrees. In a saucepan, melt margarine or butter and brown sugar. Remove from heat. Stir in eggs, biscuit mix, vanilla, and nuts. Mix well. Spread in greased 9x13-inch pan. Bake for 20 minutes. Pour Praline Frosting on top while warm. Cool. Cut into bars. Yield: 16–20 bars.

Praline Frosting

$1/2$	CUP MARGARINE OR BUTTER
1	CUP BROWN SUGAR
$1/3$	CUP WHOLE MILK
$1/2$	TEASPOON VANILLA
$1/2$	CUP PECAN PIECES
2	CUPS CONFECTIONER'S SUGAR

In a saucepan, bring margarine or butter and brown sugar to a boil. Add milk, vanilla, and pecans, and bring to another boil. Remove from heat. Stir in confectioner's sugar. Continue stirring until thickened. Pour over pecan chews.

Butter or margarine? Some cooks swear by the fresh taste of butter in their baking. Others don't care which one they use in their cooking, and often choose the much lower cost of margarine. Is either one healthier for us? The facts are that both are 100 percent fat. Margarine is made of vegetable oil and butter is an animal fat containing cholesterol.

Pecan Crunchies

1	EGG WHITE
1	CUP BROWN SUGAR
1	TEASPOON VANILLA
$1/4$	CUP ALL-PURPOSE FLOUR
2	CUPS PECAN HALVES

Preheat oven to 250 degrees. With a mixer, beat egg white until soft peaks form. Gradually add sugar and vanilla while beating until stiff peaks form and mixture is glossy. Carefully fold in the flour and pecans. Drop by teaspoons onto greased cookie sheet. Bake for 25 minutes. Turn off oven and leave cookies in an additional 25 minutes. Yield: 48 cookies.

Pecan Puffs

$1/2$	CUP MARGARINE OR BUTTER, SOFTENED
1	CUP BROWN SUGAR
1	EGG
1	TEASPOON VANILLA
1–2	TABLESPOONS WHOLE MILK
2	CUPS ALL-PURPOSE FLOUR
$1/2$	TEASPOON CREAM OF TARTAR
1	CUP PECANS, CHOPPED

Cream together margarine or butter and brown sugar. Add egg and vanilla, mixing well. Add remaining ingredients. Stir well. Shape dough into two 2-inch rolls. Refrigerate rolls until very cold and firm (at least 2 hours). To bake, preheat oven to 350 degrees. Slice rolls into thin slices. Bake on an ungreased cookie sheet afor 10 minutes. Decorate cookie tops with whole pecans or melted chocolate. Makes a very pretty cookie when decorated. Yield: 48 cookies.

Snowballs

1	CUP MARGARINE OR BUTTER, SOFTENED
$3/4$	CUP GRANULATED SUGAR
$3/4$	CUP CONFECTIONER'S SUGAR
1	EGG
1	TEASPOON VANILLA
$2^1/2$	CUPS ALL-PURPOSE FLOUR
1	TEASPOON CREAM OF TARTAR
1	TEASPOON BAKING SODA
1	TEASPOON SALT
1	CUP WALNUTS, GROUND
	ADDITIONAL CONFECTIONER'S SUGAR

Cream together margarine or butter, sugars, egg, and vanilla. Add dry ingredients. Mix well. Stir in nuts and chill dough for at least 2 hours. To bake, preheat oven to 400 degrees. Shape dough into 1-inch balls and bake for 8–10 minutes. Roll cookies into extra confectioner's sugar. Cool and roll again if desired. Yield: 36 snowballs.

Praline Snowballs

1	CUP MARGARINE OR BUTTER, SOFTENED
$3/4$	CUP BROWN SUGAR
$3/4$	CUP GRANULATED SUGAR
1	EGG
1	TEASPOON VANILLA
$1/2$	TEASPOON BUTTERNUT VANILLA FLAVORING
$3/4$	TEASPOON BAKING SODA
2	CUPS ALL-PURPOSE FLOUR
$1/2$	CUP PECANS, CHOPPED
	ADDITIONAL GRANULATED SUGAR FOR COATING

Preheat oven to 350 degrees. Cream together margarine or butter and sugars. Stir in egg and flavorings, mixing well. Stir in remaining ingredients. Shape into 1-inch balls and roll in granulated sugar. Bake for 12 minutes. Roll in additional sugar if desired. Yield: 36 snowballs.

Pecan Pie Bars

2	CUPS ALL-PURPOSE FLOUR
$1^1/_2$	CUPS BROWN SUGAR, DIVIDED
$1^1/_4$	CUPS MARGARINE OR BUTTER, DIVIDED
1	CUP PECANS, CHOPPED

Preheat oven to 350 degrees. Cream together 1 cup softened margarine or butter and 1 cup brown sugar. Add flour and mix well. Spread in a 13x9-inch pan. In a saucepan, combine remaining ingredients. Cook until mixture boils. Pour on top of sugar mixture. Bake for 20 minutes. Cool and cut into bars. Yield: 16–20 bars.

Lemon Praline Drops

$3/_4$	CUP MARGARINE OR BUTTER, SOFTENED
2	CUPS BROWN SUGAR
2	TABLESPOONS LEMON JUICE
1	TEASPOON LEMON RIND, GRATED
2	EGGS
2	CUPS ALL-PURPOSE FLOUR
1	CUP PECANS, CHOPPED
	CONFECTIONER'S SUGAR

Preheat oven to 350 degrees. Cream together margarine or butter and brown sugar. Add lemon juice and rind. Add eggs, mixing well. Stir in remaining ingredients. Refrigerate dough until firm. Drop by teaspoons onto a greased cookie sheet. Bake for 8–10 minutes. Let cool. Roll in confectioner's sugar. Yield: 36 drops

Upside-down Chocolate Chip Praline Brownies

$2^1/_2$ CUPS BROWN SUGAR, DIVIDED
$^3/_4$ CUP MARGARINE OR BUTTER, DIVIDED
$^1/_4$ CUP EVAPORATED MILK
$^1/_2$ CUP PECANS, CHOPPED
2   EGGS
$1^1/_2$ CUPS ALL-PURPOSE FLOUR
1   TEASPOON VANILLA
$^1/_2$ TEASPOON SALT
$^1/_2$ CUP CHOCOLATE CHIPS, ANY FLAVOR

Preheat oven to 350 degrees. In a saucepan, combine $^1/_2$ cup brown sugar, $^1/_4$ cup margarine or butter, milk, and pecans. Stir over low heat until margarine or butter is melted. Pour into an 8x8-inch greased baking pan. In a mixing bowl, cream the remaining brown sugar and remaining margarine or butter. Stir in eggs. Add flour, vanilla, salt, and chocolate chips. Spread chocolate chip mixture over pecan mixture in baking pan. Bake for 45 minutes or until toothpick inserted in center comes out clean. Cool for 10 minutes and invert onto serving plate. Cool slightly before cutting. Excellent with ice cream. Yield: 16 brownies.

*C*akes, *P*ies, & *D*esserts

CAKES

PIES

OTHER DESSERTS

Center photo: My great-grandfather, Fernand Benoit Rodrigue posing for his first Communion picture. Circa 1890.

Clockwise from left to right: Robertha Rodrigue Saizan and Charlotte Saizan. My fourth birthday party in Louisiana. Alvinette Prejean, poses for a picture dressed as Santa Claus. My father, Jim Saizan. Mardi Gras King cake. My first birthday cake. Canoes at lakeshore.

According to my mother, the people who don't eat fruitcakes and pass them on from Christmas to Christmas have never had a homemade cake like my grandmother's.

Grandma's Pecan Fruit Cake

This holiday fruitcake was a Christmas tradition. The availability of pecans or the price of the dried fruits determined what the cake consisted of.

1	CUP MARGARINE OR BUTTER, SOFTENED
1	CUP GRANULATED SUGAR
4	EGGS
2	TEASPOONS VANILLA
1	TEASPOON CINNAMON
$1/4$	TEASPOON SALT
1	TEASPOON BAKING POWDER
3	CUPS ALL-PURPOSE FLOUR
3	CUPS PECAN PIECES
$1^1/2$	CUPS DATES, CHOPPED
$1/2$	CUP CANDIED CHERRIES
$1^1/2$	CUPS RAISINS

Preheat oven to 300 degrees. Cream together margarine or butter and sugar. Add eggs, vanilla, cinnamon, salt, and baking powder, mixing well. Combine fruit and nut pieces with the flour. Fold into the creamed mixture until well combined. Pour into a tube pan and bake for 2 hours or until firm to the touch, or bake in 2 loaf pans for 1 hour. Yield: 8–10 slices per loaf or 16–20 servings for a tube pan.

Fig Cake

$1/2$ CUP VEGETABLE OIL
$1/3$ CUP GRANULATED SUGAR
2   EGGS
1   CUP ALL-PURPOSE FLOUR
1   TEASPOON VANILLA
2   TEASPOONS BAKING POWDER
$1/4$ TEASPOON SALT
$1/4$ TEASPOON BAKING SODA
$1^1/2$ CUPS FIGS, CHOPPED

Preheat oven to 350 degrees. Mix together ingredients in order listed. Bake in a greased and floured 8x8-inch baking pan for 45 minutes or until a toothpick inserted comes out clean. No need to frost. Yield: 9–12 servings.

Pecan Chocolate Chip Pound Cake

1   CUP MARGARINE OR BUTTER, SOFTENED
1   8-OUNCE PACKAGE CREAM CHEESE, SOFTENED
3   CUPS GRANULATED SUGAR
1   TEASPOON VANILLA
1   TEASPOON BUTTERNUT VANILLA FLAVORING
$1/4$ TEASPOON SALT
3   EGGS
$1/2$ TEASPOON BAKING POWDER
3   CUPS ALL-PURPOSE FLOUR
2   CUPS CHOCOLATE CHIPS, RESERVING 1 TABLESPOON
1   CUP PECANS, CHOPPED, RESERVING 1 TABLESPOON

Preheat oven to 325 degrees. Cream together margarine or butter, cream cheese, and sugar. Stir in flavorings and salt. Add eggs, beating well. Stir in remaining ingredients, reserving 1 tablespoon each of chocolate chips and pecans. With reserve, sprinkle in the bottom of a greased and floured bundt pan. Pour batter in pan. Bake for 2 hours or until cake is firm. Cool cake before inverting. Serve plain or with praline sauce drizzled over (see p. 120). Yield: 16–20 servings.

Praline Sauce

1   CUP DARK CORN SYRUP
$1/_8$ CUP BROWN SUGAR
3   TABLESPOONS WATER
$1/_2$ TEASPOON VANILLA
$1/_2$ CUP PECANS, CHOPPED

In a saucepan combine the corn syrup, brown sugar, and water. Bring to a boil and continue to boil for one minute. Remove from heat and stir in vanilla and pecans. Drizzle warm sauce over cake.

Praline Apple Cake

1   CUP VEGETABLE OIL
2   CUPS GRANULATED SUGAR
3   EGGS, BEATEN
$1^1/_2$ TEASPOONS VANILLA
$2^1/_3$ CUPS ALL-PURPOSE FLOUR
2   TEASPOONS BAKING POWDER
1   TEASPOON BAKING SODA
1   TEASPOON CINNAMON
1   TEASPOON SALT
3   CUPS APPLES, PEELED AND CHOPPED
1   CUP PECANS, CHOPPED

Preheat oven to 350 degrees. In a large mixing bowl, cream together oil, sugar, eggs, and vanilla. Stir in dry ingredients, mixing until smooth. Fold in apples and pecans. Pour into a greased and floured bundt pan. Bake for 50–55 minutes or until firm. Invert cake and cool. Drizzle praline glaze over before serving. Yield: 16–20 servings.

Praline Glaze

1   CUP BROWN SUGAR
$1/_2$ CUP MARGARINE OR BUTTER
$1/_2$ CUP EVAPORATED MILK
1   TEASPOON VANILLA

In a small saucepan, heat brown sugar, margarine or butter, and milk until boiling. Heat while stirring continuously. Remove from heat and stir in vanilla, stirring until slightly thickened. Cool glaze and drizzle over cake.

Mardi Gras is observed exactly forty-seven days preceding Easter: forty days of Lent and seven Sundays. It can occur between February 3 and March 9. Mardi Gras means "fat Tuesday." It's the last day to indulge in fat before Lent. Mardi Gras celebrations begin on Epiphany, twelve days after Christmas. This was the day the wise men visited the baby Jesus. The King Cake celebrates this occasion with the symbolic decorative colors on the cake. Purple for justice, green for faith, and gold for power. Inside the cake is a hidden plastic baby. The person receiving the surprise in their piece of cake will have good luck for the rest of the year. They are also to furnish the next cake at the next party.

Mardi Gras King Cake

1	$1/4$-OUNCE PACKAGE YEAST
$1/4$	CUP WARM WATER
$1/4$	CUP WHOLE MILK
$1/4$	CUP GRANULATED SUGAR
$1/2$	TEASPOON SALT
3	TABLESPOONS MARGARINE OR BUTTER
1	EGG, BEATEN
$2^{1}/4$	CUPS ALL-PURPOSE FLOUR
$1/4$	CUP MARGARINE OR BUTTER, MELTED
$1/2$	CUP GRANULATED SUGAR AND 1 TEASPOON CINNAMON, MIXED
1	MINIATURE PLASTIC BABY OR 1 DRIED BEAN

In a small bowl, dissolve yeast in warm water. Set aside. In a saucepan, scald milk and sugar. Remove from heat and add salt and 3 tablespoon margarine or butter. Cool to lukewarm and add yeast and egg. Stir in flour. Turn out on a well-floured surface. Cover and let rise until doubled. Place on a floured surface and roll out to a rectangular shape. Spread with melted margarine or butter and sprinkle on cinnamon sugar mixture. Place baby or dried bean on dough. Begin rolling as you would a jelly roll. Seal the edges so the cake makes a ring. Place on a greased baking sheet and bake at 375 degrees for 13 to 15 minutes or until golden. Ice with Confectioner's Glaze after cake is cooled (see p. 122). Yield: 12–16 servings.

Confectioner's Glaze

$1^1/_2$ CUPS CONFECTIONER'S SUGAR
3   TABLESPOONS WHOLE MILK
$^1/_2$ TEASPOON VANILLA OR OTHER FLAVORING

Mix together ingredients and divide icing into 3 parts. Tint parts with green, yellow, and purple. Drizzle over King Cake. Add colored sprinkles if desired.

Praline Cheesecake

$1^1/_4$ CUPS GRAHAM CRACKER CRUMBS
$^1/_4$ CUP GRANULATED SUGAR
$^1/_4$ CUP PECANS, CHOPPED
$^1/_4$ CUP MARGARINE OR BUTTER, MELTED
3   8-OUNCE PACKAGES CREAM CHEESE, SOFTENED
1   CUP BROWN SUGAR
1   5-OUNCE CAN EVAPORATED MILK
2   TABLESPOONS ALL-PURPOSE FLOUR
$1^1/_2$ TEASPOONS VANILLA
3   EGGS
1   CUP PECAN HALVES, TOASTED

Preheat oven to 250 degrees. Toast pecan halves for 10 minutes. Remove and set aside. Increase oven temperature to 350 degrees. In a small bowl, combine cracker crumbs, granulated sugar, and chopped pecans. Stir the melted margarine or butter into the mixture. Press crumb mixture over the bottom and an inch or so up the sides of a 9-inch springform pan. Bake for 10 minutes. Meanwhile, combine softened cream cheese, brown sugar, evaporated milk, flour, and vanilla, mixing until smooth. Add eggs, beating well after each egg is added. Pour into baked crust. Bake for 50–55 minutes or set. Cool in pan for approximately 30 minutes. Loosen sides and remove rim from pan. Cool completely. Arrange pecan halves atop cheesecake. Before serving, combine 1 cup dark corn syrup, $^1/_4$ cup cornstarch, and 2 tablespoons brown sugar in a small saucepan. Cook and stir until thick and bubbly. Stir in 1 teaspoon vanilla. Cool. Spoon the warm sauce over the cheesecake before serving. Yield: 12–16 servings.

Mini Cheesecakes

3   8-OUNCE PACKAGES CREAM CHEESE, SOFTENED
1   CUP GRANULATED SUGAR
5   EGGS
1   TEASPOON VANILLA

Preheat oven to 325 degrees. Mix all ingredients until smooth. Pour batter $2/3$ full into greased mini muffin cups. Bake for 30–35 minutes or until firm. Remove and top with chocolate chips while cheesecakes are still warm. A dollop of fruit preserves also makes a good topping. These mini cheesecakes are just the right size for snacking. Yield: 48 mini-cheesecakes.

Four-layer Coconut Sour Cream Cake

I'm told that our great Aunt Rena made the best Coconut Cake from scratch. This recipe from Eleanor Saizan Thibodeaux isn't entirely from scratch, but it is the best coconut cake I've ever run across. I think you'll agree!

1       $18^1/_4$-OUNCE BOX WHITE CAKE MIX
1   TEASPOON COCONUT FLAVORING
2   CUPS GRANULATED SUGAR
1   16-OUNCE CONTAINER OF SOUR CREAM
1   6-OUNCE BAG COCONUT (RESERVE $^1/_2$ CUP)
1   8-OUNCE CONTAINER OF WHIPPED TOPPING
$1^1/_2$ ADDITIONAL TEASPOONS COCONUT FLAVORING

Mix white cake mix according to directions. Stir in 1 teaspoon coconut flavoring. Bake in two greased and floured 9-inch cake pans. Bake according to directions. Cool for 10 minutes and invert cakes from pans. With heavy string, cut each layer in half so that you have 4 layers. Meanwhile, combine sugar, sour cream, coconut (reserving $^1/_2$ cup), and 1 teaspoon coconut flavoring. Spread 1 cup of this mixture between the cake layers. With remaining mixture, stir in cool whip and the remaining $^1/_2$ teaspoon coconut flavoring and ice the sides and top of cake. Sprinkle remaining $^1/_2$ cup coconut on top and sides. Refrigerate in a cake keeper and do not touch for 3 days. The longer the cake sits, the more intense the flavor. Yield: 16–20 servings.

According to family members, my great-great-grandmother, Azelie Gonsulin, and her family were from French nobility and were personal friends of the king of Spain. Upon their arrival in Louisiana, the Gonsulins were given grants of land from the king, including the tract of land known as Belle Isle near the Gulf Coast. With relatives representing just about all of the Gulf Coast states, I thought it would be fun to include these five Gulf Coast cake recipes that I've run across over the years. All are truly delicious, unique, southern desserts.

Florida Sunshine Cake

2	CUPS ALL-PURPOSE FLOUR
$2^1/_2$	TEASPOONS BAKING POWDER
$3/_4$	TEASPOON SALT
$2/_3$	CUP SHORTENING
$1^1/_2$	CUPS GRANULATED SUGAR
1	TABLESPOON ORANGE PEEL, GRATED
2	TEASPOONS LEMON PEEL, GRATED
3	EGGS
$1/_3$	CUP ORANGE JUICE, FRESH OR CARTON
$1/_3$	CUP WHOLE MILK

Preheat oven to 350 degrees. With a mixer, beat shortening, sugar, and peels for 1 minute or until well blended. Add eggs one at a time, beating after each. Add the dry ingredients alternately with the juice and milk, beating well after each addition. Pour batter into 2 greased and floured 9-inch round cake pans. Bake for 30 minutes or until toothpick inserted comes out clean. Cool for 10 minutes and invert cake. Fill layers with Fruit Filling and frost with Fluffy White Frosting. Yield: 12–16 servings.

FRUIT FILLING:

1	EGG, BEATEN
1	CUP GRANULATED SUGAR
2	TABLESPOONS CORNSTARCH
1	TABLESPOON VANILLA
$1^1/_4$	CUPS WHOLE MILK
$3/_4$	CUP FRUIT, CHOPPED OR MASHED

In a small saucepan, scald milk. Set aside. In a mixing bowl, cream together remaining ingredients except fruit. Gradually pour milk into the creamed mixture, stirring continuously. Cool and stir in fruit. Spread between cake layers and frost with fluffy white frosting. Bananas and drained, crushed pineapple work best in this recipe.

Fluffy White Frosting

1	CUP GRANULATED SUGAR
$1/3$	CUP WATER
	DASH OF SALT
$1/2$	TEASPOON CREAM OF TARTAR
2	EGG WHITES
1	TEASPOON VANILLA

In a saucepan, cook the sugar, water, salt, and cream of tartar until sugar dissolves. Bring to a boil, and boil for 4 minutes. In a mixing bowl, combine the egg whites and vanilla. With a mixer, begin beating egg whites on high speed while gradually adding sugar. Slowly pour sugar mixture over unbeaten egg whites. Mix on high speed for several minutes or until stiff peaks form.

Alabama Pea Pickin' Cake

1	$18^1/4$-OUNCE BOX BUTTER CAKE MIX
3	EGGS
$1/2$	CUP VEGETABLE OIL
$3/4$	CUP ORANGE JUICE
1	14-OUNCE CAN MANDARIN ORANGES, DRAINED

ICING:

1	12-OUNCE CONTAINER OF WHIPPED TOPPING
1	15-OUNCE CAN OF CRUSHED PINEAPPLES WITH JUICE
1	5-OUNCE VANILLA INSTANT PUDDING MIX

Preheat oven to 350 degrees. With an electric mixer on medium speed, combine cake mix, eggs, vegetable oil, and juice until smooth. Fold in drained oranges. Bake in 2 greased and floured 8-inch cake pans for 30 minutes or until toothpick inserted comes out clean. Cool for 10 minutes and invert cake layers. Combine icing ingredients. Spread between layers and on outside of cake. Refrigerate and serve chilled. Yield: 12–16 servings.

Mississippi Mud Cake

1	CUP MARGARINE OR BUTTER, SOFTENED
2	CUPS GRANULATED SUGAR
4	EGGS
$1^1/_2$	TEASPOONS VANILLA
$1^1/_2$	CUPS ALL-PURPOSE FLOUR
1	TEASPOON BAKING SODA
$^1/_4$	TEASPOON SALT
$^1/_2$	CUP COCOA
1	$10^1/_2$-OUNCE BAG MINIATURE MARSHMALLOWS
1	CUP PECANS, CHOPPED
$1^1/_2$	TEASPOONS CHOCOLATE LIQUEUR

Preheat oven to 350 degrees. Cream together margarine or butter and sugar. Add eggs, vanilla, and liqueur, mixing well. Stir in dry ingredients. Pour into a greased and floured 9x13 inch pan. Bake for approximately 40 minutes or until toothpick inserted comes out clean. Remove from oven and sprinkle marshmallows over warm cake. Sprinkle pecans on top. Pour icing over. Yield: 16–20 servings.

ICING:

$^1/_2$	CUP MARGARINE OR BUTTER
$^1/_2$	CUP COCOA
$^1/_2$	CUP WHOLE MILK
$^1/_2$	TEASPOON VANILLA
1	16-OUNCE BOX CONFECTIONER'S SUGAR
$^1/_2$	TEASPOON CHOCOLATE LIQUEUR

In a saucepan, bring margarine or butter, cocoa, milk, and flavorings to a boil. Remove from heat and stir in confectioner's sugar. Spread over cake. Top with additional pecans if desired.

Texas Sheet Cake

This unique Texas sheet cake recipe comes from the collection of my brother and sister-in-law, Jim and Pat Saizan. Pat loves to cook and collect recipes. This is one of her favorites and mine, too!

2	CUPS GRANULATED SUGAR
2	CUPS ALL-PURPOSE FLOUR
$1/2$	CUP MARGARINE OR BUTTER
$1/2$	CUP SHORTENING
$1/4$	CUP COCOA
1	CUP WATER
$1/2$	CUP BUTTERMILK
1	TEASPOON CINNAMON (OPTIONAL)
1	TEASPOON BAKING SODA
1	TEASPOON VANILLA
2	EGGS

Preheat oven to 350 degrees. In a large mixing bowl, combine sugar and flour. Set aside. In a saucepan, heat margarine or butter, shortening, cocoa, and water to boiling. Pour over sugar and flour, mixing well. Stir in remaining ingredients. Pour into a greased and floured 9x13-inch pan. Bake for 20 minutes or until toothpick inserted comes out clean. Pour frosting over while cake is still warm. Yield: 16–20 servings.

FROSTING:

$1/2$	CUP MARGARINE OR BUTTER
$1/4$	CUP EVAPORATED MILK
$1/4$	CUP COCOA
2	CUPS CONFECTIONER'S SUGAR
1	TEASPOON VANILLA
1	CUP PECAN PIECES

Combine margarine or butter, milk, cocoa, and confectioner's sugar in saucepan and bring to a boil. Use a wire whisk to remove lumps. Stir in remaining ingredients. Pour over warm cake.

Louisiana Yam Cake

Opelousas, Louisiana, is known as the yam capitol of the United States. Lurline Rodrigue Duplechain lived there and created this award-winning Louisiana Yam Cake.

1	CUP MARGARINE OR BUTTER, SOFTENED
2	CUPS GRANULATED SUGAR
$1/2$	TEASPOON BUTTER EXTRACT
$2^1/_2$	CUPS YAMS, COOKED AND MASHED
4	EGGS
3	CUPS ALL-PURPOSE FLOUR
$1/4$	TEASPOON SALT
2	TEASPOONS BAKING POWDER
1	TEASPOON BAKING SODA
1	TEASPOON CINNAMON
$1/2$	TEASPOON NUTMEG
1	TEASPOON VANILLA
1	TEASPOON LEMON EXTRACT
$1/2$	CUP PECANS, CHOPPED
$1/2$	CUP FLAKED COCONUT
1	ENVELOPE DREAM WHIP, MIXED ACCORDING TO DIRECTIONS

Preheat oven to 350 degrees. With a mixer, cream together margarine or butter, sugar, and butter extract. Add the yams and beat until light and fluffy. Add eggs one at a time, beating well after each. Add the dry ingredients, mixing well. Fold in remaining extracts, pecans, and coconut. Spread batter in 3 greased and floured 9-inch cake pans. Bake for 35 minutes or until a toothpick inserted comes out clean. Cool for 10 minutes and invert cake layers. Spread with whipped topping between and on top of layers. Garnish with additional pecans if desired. Cake tastes best when it's a day or so old because flavors become more intense. Yield: 16–20 servings.

What are the differences between sweet potatoes and yams? One source says yams are the bigger of the sweet potato crop. Another says the distinction is simply a marketing strategy. In fact, sweet potatoes are tuberous roots that are related to the morning glory plant. Yams are also tuberous roots. They are lighter in color and not as tender or as sweet as sweet potatoes. The two are often used interchangeably in recipes.

Sweet Potato Spice Cake

$1^1/_2$	CUPS VEGETABLE OIL
2	CUPS GRANULATED SUGAR
3	EGGS, SEPARATED
$1/_4$	CUP HOT WATER
1	TEASPOON VANILLA
$2^1/_2$	CUPS ALL-PURPOSE FLOUR
3	TEASPOONS BAKING POWDER
$1/_4$	TEASPOON SALT
$1/_2$	TEASPOON ALLSPICE
$1/_2$	TEASPOON NUTMEG
2	TEASPOONS CINNAMON
1	CUP PECANS, CHOPPED
2	CUPS SWEET POTATOES, COOKED AND MASHED **OR**
1	$15^1/_2$-OUNCE CAN SWEET POTATOES, DRAINED

Preheat oven to 350 degrees. Beat oil and sugar together. Add egg yolks, water, and vanilla, mixing well. Stir in the dry ingredients including spices, then the pecans and sweet potatoes. Beat egg whites with a mixer until soft peaks form. Fold into cake batter. Pour batter into 2 greased and floured 9-inch cake pans. Bake for 35–40 minutes or until a toothpick inserted comes out clean. Cool for 10 minutes and invert cake layers. Frost with cream cheese frosting. Garnish with additional pecans if desired. Yield: 12–16 servings.

Cream Cheese Frosting

1	8-OUNCE PACKAGE CREAM CHEESE, SOFTENED
$1/_2$	CUP MARGARINE OR BUTTER, SOFTENED
1	TEASPOON VANILLA
1	16-OUNCE BOX CONFECTIONER'S SUGAR

Cream together softened cream cheese, margarine or butter, and vanilla. Gradually stir in sugar until it reaches a creamy, spreading consistency. Spread frosting between layers and on top of cake.

The recipes for Black Walnut Cake and Persimmon Cake are contributed by my mother-in-law, Nell Williams Corbin. She remembers her grandmother, Flora, always having a dessert in the pie safe. This Black Walnut Cake recipe is similar to the hickory nut cake she remembers Flora making.

Black Walnut Cake

1	CUP MARGARINE OR BUTTER
2	CUPS GRANULATED SUGAR
3	EGGS, SEPARATED
2	CUPS ALL-PURPOSE FLOUR
$2^1/_2$	TEASPOONS BAKING POWDER
1	CUP WALNUT PIECES
1	CUP WHOLE MILK
1	TEASPOON VANILLA

Preheat oven to 350 degrees. Cream together margarine or butter and sugar. Stir in egg yolks and vanilla. Add dry ingredients alternately with milk. Stir in walnuts. In a small bowl, beat egg whites until stiff peaks form. Fold into cake batter. Pour into 2 greased and floured 9-inch cake pans. Bake for 35–40 minutes or until toothpick inserted comes out clean. Cool for 10 minutes and invert. Frost with Fluffy White Frosting (see p. 125) or Praline Frosting (see p. 111). Hickory nuts may be substituted for the walnuts. Yield: 12–16 servings.

Persimmon Cake

$3/_4$	CUP MARGARINE OR BUTTER
2	CUPS GRANULATED SUGAR
1	EGG
$1^3/_4$	CUPS ALL-PURPOSE FLOUR
1	TEASPOON BAKING SODA
1	TEASPOON CINNAMON
1	TEASPOON CLOVES
1	CUP RAISINS
1	CUP PECAN PIECES
1	CUP PERSIMMON PULP

Preheat oven to 350 degrees. Cream together margarine or butter, sugar, and egg, mixing well. Sift dry ingredients together. Add raisins and pecans. Alternate adding the persimmon pulp and the dry ingredients to the sugar mixture. Pour into a greased and floured 9x13 pan. Bake for 35–40 minutes or until toothpick inserted comes out clean. Yield: 12–16 servings.

Persimmons were brought to America from Asia in the sixteenth century. A tree fruit that is orange in color, the persimmon should be eaten ripe or overripe. If not, it puckers the lips and is very bitter on the tongue. The fruit can be eaten right from the tree, or made into a pulp to be used in cake and pie recipes, such as this Persimmon Cake.

Grandma's Homemade Yellow Cake

$2/3$ CUP MARGARINE OR BUTTER, SOFTENED
$1^3/4$ CUPS GRANULATED SUGAR
2   EGGS
1   TEASPOON VANILLA
3   CUPS ALL-PURPOSE FLOUR, SIFTED
1   TABLESPOON BAKING SODA
1   TEASPOON SALT
$1^1/4$ CUPS WHOLE MILK

Preheat oven to 350 degrees. With a mixer, beat margarine or butter, sugar, eggs, and vanilla on high for 5 minutes. Add sifted dry ingredients alternately with milk, beating well after each addition. Pour batter into 2 greased and floured 9-inch round cake pans. Bake for 35–40 minutes or until a toothpick inserted comes out clean. Cool for 10 minutes before inverting. Spread layers with Fruit Filling (see p. 124) and frost with your favorite frosting. For birthday cake, frost with Bakery Frosting (see p. 132). Yield: 12–16 servings.

Bakery Frosting

1	POUND CONFECTIONER'S SUGAR
$1/2$	CUP VEGETABLE SHORTENING
$1/4$	CUP WHOLE MILK
2–3	TABLESPOONS LEMON JUICE

Combine ingredients with a mixer until a spreading consistency is reached. For decorative flowers and borders, decrease milk slightly.

Grandma's Layer Jelly Cake

This is a very old recipe that my grandmother used to make.

Follow directions for Grandma's Homemade Yellow Cake (see p. 131). Divide batter in sixths, and bake in greased and floured pans. Bake for 7–10 minutes or until toothpick inserted comes out clean. The cakes will be about an inch or so thick after baking. Spread with your favorite jelly in between layers. Sprinkle with confectioner's sugar before serving.

This layer cake recipe is reminiscent of the old fashioned wedding cakes where guests would bring their own cake layers and filling to add to the wedding cake. The taller the wedding cake, the more popular the bride.

Award Winning Lemon-Lime Soda Cake

The Lemon-Lime Soda Cake is another winning recipe by my cousin, Lurline Rodrigue Duplechain.

1	$18^{1}/_{4}$-OUNCE BOX LEMON SUPREME CAKE MIX
1	3-OUNCE BOX VANILLA INSTANT PUDDING
4	EGGS
$3/4$	CUP VEGETABLE OIL
1	CUP LEMON-LIME SODA

Preheat oven to 300 degrees. With a mixer, combine all ingredients, mixing well. Pour batter in two 9-inch greased and floured cake pans. Bake for 35 minutes or until a toothpick inserted comes out clean. Cool for 10 minutes and invert; fill layers and frost cake with Filling. Yield: 12–16 servings.

FILLING:

2	EGGS, BEATEN
2	TABLESPOONS ALL-PURPOSE FLOUR
$1^1/_2$	CUPS GRANULATED SUGAR
$^1/_2$	CUP MARGARINE OR BUTTER
1	CUP FLAKED COCONUT
1	15-OZ. CAN PINEAPPLE, CRUSHED WITH JUICE

Combine eggs, flour, and sugar. Add remaining ingredients. Cook over low heat until thick. Cool and spread between layers of cake and on the outside of cake. Refrigerate and serve chilled.

In the South, all flavors of sodas are called cokes. It is very common to order a coke in a restaurant and have the waitress ask, "What kind of coke?"

Chocolate Cola Cake

Carbonated beverages made their way into desserts about fifty or so years ago. This Chocolate Cola Cake is the most recent I've come across.

2	CUPS ALL-PURPOSE FLOUR
1	CUP GRANULATED SUGAR
1	CUP MARGARINE OR BUTTER
$^1/_4$	CUP COCOA
1	CUP COLA
$^1/_2$	CUP BUTTERMILK
2	EGGS, BEATEN
1	TEASPOON BAKING SODA
1	TEASPOON VANILLA

Preheat oven to 350 degrees. In a mixing bowl, combine the flour and sugar. Set aside. In a saucepan, combine margarine or butter, cocoa, and Coca-Cola. Bring to a boil. Pour liquid over flour and sugar mixture, stirring well. Add remaining ingredients. Pour into a greased and floured 9x13 pan. Bake for 35–40 minutes or until toothpick inserted comes out clean. Cool and frost with chocolate butter cream frosting. Yield: 12–16 servings.

Chocolate Butter Cream Frosting

$1/2$ CUP MARGARINE OR BUTTER
$2/3$ CUP COCOA
3   CUPS CONFECTIONER'S SUGAR
$1/3$ CUP EVAPORATED MILK
$1/2$ TEASPOON VANILLA

In a saucepan, melt margarine or butter. Stir in cocoa. Add confectioner's sugar alternately with milk until smooth. Stir in vanilla. Cool completely. Yield: 2 cups.

Syrup Cake

According to my mother, my great-grandfather had a cane syrup business. He grew cane sugar and also made and sold the syrup. This cake is an authentic early southern cake typical of what my great-grandmother made.

1   CUP SHORTENING
1   CUP GRANULATED SUGAR
$1^1/2$ CUPS CANE SYRUP
3   EGGS
1   CUP WHOLE MILK
3   CUPS ALL-PURPOSE FLOUR
$1^1/2$ TEASPOONS BAKING SODA
1   TEASPOON CINNAMON
1   TEASPOON ALLSPICE
$1/2$ TEASPOON SALT

Preheat oven to 350 degrees. Cream together shortening and sugar. Add syrup and eggs. Mix well. Add dry ingredients alternately with the milk. Pour batter into a greased and floured 9x13 pan. Bake for approximately 40 to 45 minutes or until toothpick inserted comes out clean. Yield: 16–20 servings.

Perfect Piecrust

A perfect pie begins with a perfect piecrust. The majority of the pies in this section are from my mother Charlotte Sundberg Saizan's recipe collection. They are some of the best pies you'll ever eat.

1	CUP ALL-PURPOSE FLOUR
$1/3$	CUP SOLID VEGETABLE SHORTENING
$1/4$	TEASPOON SALT
3–4	TABLESPOONS ICE WATER

Preheat oven to 375 degrees. With a pastry blender, cut shortening and salt into flour until the mixture resembles coarse meal. Stir in 3–4 tablespoons ice water until mixture forms a ball (use your hands if necessary). Roll out dough on a floured surface, large enough to cover your pie plate. Lift carefully and press in pie plate. Trim and flute edges if desired. Bake for 12–15 minutes or until lightly browned. Handle as little as possible for a flakier crust. Yield: one 9-inch piecrust.

Mini Pecan Tarts

CRUST:

1	3-OUNCE PACKAGE CREAM CHEESE
1	TABLESPOON MARGARINE OR BUTTER, MELTED
1	CUP ALL-PURPOSE FLOUR

Cream together cream cheese, margarine or butter, and flour. Divide dough into 24 balls, pressing each onto the bottom and sides of each space of a mini muffin pan.

FILLING:

$1/2$	CUP MARGARINE OR BUTTER
$3/4$	CUP BROWN SUGAR
1	EGG, BEATEN
1	TEASPOON VANILLA
1	CUP PECAN HALVES

Preheat oven to 350 degrees. Cream together softened margarine or butter and sugar. Stir in egg and vanilla. Spoon by teaspoonful into each crust. Top with pecans. Bake for 15 minutes. Reduce heat to 250 degrees for an additional 15 minutes or until golden brown. Yield: 24 tarts.

My mother's parents had a pecan orchard and almost always had a dessert around with pecans in it. Grandma's Pecan Pie recipe is thought to be almost one hundred years old. Grandma Mamie's pronunciation of pecans was with a long e, sounding like pea can. *Depending on where in the South you were from certainly influenced your accent, your slang, nicknames, and enunciation.*

Grandma's Pecan Pie

3	TABLESPOONS BUTTER, SOFTENED
$^2/_3$	CUP BROWN SUGAR
3	EGGS
1	TEASPOON VANILLA
$^1/_2$	CUP LIGHT CORN SYRUP
$^1/_2$	CUP WHOLE MILK
1	CUP WHOLE PECANS
	UNBAKED PIE SHELL

Preheat oven to 375 degrees. In a mixing bowl, cream together butter and sugar. Add eggs, beating well after each. Stir in remaining ingredients. Pour into an unbaked 9-inch pie shell and bake for approximately 40–45 minutes. Yield: 8 servings.

Sweet Potato Pie

3	CUPS SWEET POTATOES, COOKED AND MASHED
1	CUP GRANULATED SUGAR
$^1/_2$	CUP MARGARINE OR BUTTER
2	TEASPOONS VANILLA
$^1/_2$	TEASPOON LEMON FLAVORING (OPTIONAL)

Preheat oven to 350 degrees. After cooking and mashing sweet potatoes, mix with a mixer to remove lumps. Stir in remaining ingredients. Pour into an unbaked 9-inch pie shell and bake for 40 minutes. Delicious warm or cold. For variety, lemon flavoring may be added. Yield: 8 servings.

Blackberry Pie

The next two fruit pies are contributions from my cousin Lurline Rodrigue Duplechain. Lurline has contributed many recipes to local cookbooks and has won awards for her recipes. No doubt these two pies are also winners!

3	TABLESPOONS ALL-PURPOSE FLOUR, SIFTED
1	CUP GRANULATED SUGAR
3	CUPS BLACKBERRIES
3	TABLESPOONS BUTTER
2	UNBAKED 9-INCH PIE SHELLS

Preheat oven to 400 degrees. Combine flour and sugar. Add this to the blackberries. Pour into an unbaked pie shell and dot the mixture with the butter. Cover with the other pie shell or pie dough lattice. Bake for 15 minutes. Reduce temperature to 350 degrees and continue baking until crust is golden brown or 30–45 minutes. Serve with whipped topping or ice cream if desired. Yield: 8 servings.

Pear Pie

$1/2$	CUP MARGARINE OR BUTTER, MELTED
2	TABLESPOONS LEMON JUICE
4	CUPS PEARS, PEELED AND SLICED
1	CUP GRANULATED SUGAR
2	TABLESPOONS ALL-PURPOSE FLOUR
$1/2$	TEASPOON CINNAMON
2	UNBAKED 9-INCH PIE SHELLS

Pour margarine or butter and lemon juice over pears. Toss. Add sugar, flour, and cinnamon. Toss until well coated. Pour mixture into one pie shell and use the other to cover the top. Seal edges with a fork. Cut slits on top of crust. Place on a cookie sheet and bake approximately one hour at 350 degrees. Serve with ice cream or whipped topping. Yield: 8 servings.

Chocolate Meringue Pie

$3/4$ CUP GRANULATED SUGAR
$1/3$ CUP ALL-PURPOSE FLOUR
$1/4$ CUP COCOA
        DASH OF SALT
$2^1/2$ CUPS WHOLE MILK
2   EGGS, SEPARATED
1   TEASPOON VANILLA
1   9-INCH PIECRUST, BAKED

Preheat oven to 350 degrees. Combine sugar, flour, cocoa, salt, and milk in a saucepan. Cook over medium heat, stirring constantly. Meanwhile separate eggs. Stir a small amount of hot mixture into the egg yolks. Add yolk mixture to saucepan, cooking until thick and bubbly. Remove from heat and stir in vanilla. Pour chocolate mixture into baked piecrust. Meanwhile, with a mixer, beat egg whites on high. Gradually stir in 2 tablespoons of sugar. Continue beating until stiff peaks form. Spread meringue on top of pie. Bake for 8–10 minutes or until meringue begins to brown. Yield: 8 servings.

Coconut Meringue Pie

$2/3$ CUP PLUS 2 TABLESPOONS GRANULATED SUGAR
$1/3$ CUP ALL-PURPOSE FLOUR
        DASH OF SALT
1   TEASPOON VANILLA
$2^1/2$ CUPS WHOLE MILK
2   EGGS, SEPARATED
$2/3$ CUP FLAKED COCONUT
1   9-INCH PIECRUST, BAKED

Preheat oven to 350 degrees. Combine $2/3$ cup sugar, flour, salt, and milk in a saucepan. Cook over medium heat, stirring constantly. Stir a small amount of hot mixture into the egg yolks. Add yolk mixture to saucepan, stirring well. Continue cooking until thick and bubbly. Remove from heat. Cool slightly. Stir in half the coconut and pour mixture into pie shell. Meanwhile, beat the egg whites on high with an electric mixer, gradually adding 2 tablespoons of sugar. Beat until stiff peaks form. Pour meringue on top of pie and sprinkle with remaining coconut. Bake for 10 minutes or until lightly browned. Yield: 8 servings.

Banana Meringue Pie

1	9-INCH PIECRUST, BAKED
1	LARGE BANANA, SLICED
$2/3$	CUP PLUS 2 TABLESPOONS GRANULATED SUGAR
$1/3$	CUP ALL-PURPOSE FLOUR
	DASH OF SALT
1	TEASPOON VANILLA
$2^1/2$	CUPS WHOLE MILK
2	EGGS, SEPARATED

Preheat oven to 350 degrees. Layer banana slices on the bottom of crust. Combine $2/3$ cup sugar, flour, salt, vanilla, and milk in a saucepan. Cook over medium heat stirring constantly. Stir a small amount of hot mixture into the egg yolks. Add yolk mixture to saucepan, cooking until thick and bubbly. Remove from heat. Cool slightly. Pour pudding mixture into crust. Meanwhile, beat egg whites with a mixer. Gradually add the 2 tablespoons of sugar. Beat until stiff peaks form. Spread over pie. Bake for 10 minutes or until meringue is golden brown. Yield: 8 servings.

Loaf Bread Pudding

Bread pudding is an excellent way of using up leftover breads. This recipe comes from my family's collection and has been around for many, many years. It can be eaten alone or is complemented by the Praline Sauce on page 120.

2	TABLESPOONS MARGARINE OR BUTTER, MELTED
12	BREAD SLICES
1	CUP GRANULATED SUGAR
2	EGGS, BEATEN
$2^1/4$	CUP WHOLE MILK
2	TEASPOONS VANILLA
$1/3$	CUP RAISINS

Preheat oven to 350 degrees. Pour melted margarine or butter into a loaf pan. Set aside. In a mixing bowl, tear bread into small pieces and combine with remaining ingredients. Mix well. Pour into loaf pan and bake for 50 minutes. Cut into slices to serve. Sprinkle with cinnamon sugar if desired. Yield: 8–10 servings.

Basic Fruit Cobbler

$^1/_2$ CUP MARGARINE OR BUTTER, MELTED
1   CUP GRANULATED SUGAR
1   CUP WHOLE MILK
1   CUP SELF-RISING FLOUR
3   CUPS FRESH FRUIT, OR 1 28-OZ. CANNED FRUIT

Preheat oven to 350 degrees. Mix together margarine or butter, sugar, milk, flour, and fruit and pour into a greased baking dish. Bake for 40 minutes. Yield: 6–8 servings.

Basic Shortcakes

$^1/_3$ CUP SHORTENING
2   CUPS ALL-PURPOSE FLOUR
2   TABLESPOONS GRANULATED SUGAR
1   TABLESPOON BAKING POWDER
$^1/_2$ TEASPOON SALT
$^3/_4$ CUP WHOLE MILK
     MARGARINE OR BUTTER

Preheat oven to 425 degrees. In a mixing bowl, cut shortening into the flour, sugar, baking powder, and salt until mixture is crumbly. Stir in the milk until well blended. Turn dough onto a floured surface and knead for approximately 1 minute. Roll dough to a $^1/_2$-inch thickness. With a large glass, cut circles into dough. Place circles on a greased cookie sheet and bake for approximately 10 minutes or until golden brown. Split shortcakes and spread margarine or butter between layers. Fill layer with fruit of your choice and whipped cream. Top cakes with additional fruit and whipped cream if desired. Yield: 8–10 shortcakes.

Mama's Jelly Roll

$3/4$	TEASPOON BAKING POWDER
$1/4$	TEASPOON SALT
4	EGGS (AT ROOM TEMPERATURE)
1	TEASPOON VANILLA
$3/4$	CUP GRANULATED SUGAR
$3/4$	CUP ALL-PURPOSE FLOUR
	CONFECTIONER'S SUGAR
1	CUP FRUIT PRESERVES

In a mixing bowl, combine baking powder, salt, eggs, and vanilla and beat with electric mixer, adding granulated sugar gradually until mixture becomes thick. Fold in the flour by hand. Pour in a jelly-roll pan that has been lined with greased wax paper. Bake at 400 degrees for 13 minutes. Turn out onto paper towels that have been dusted with confectioner's sugar. Spread with your favorite fruit preserves. Roll up and slice to serve. Sprinkle with additional confectioner's sugar if desired. Yield: 8–10 servings.

Cranberry Cream Cheese Dessert

A school cafeteria manager for many years, Doris Hancock contributed this delicious cranberry dessert. It was a traditional dish she took to church potluck dinners, and it was always a hit!

1	CUP HOT WATER
1	15-OUNCE CAN CRANBERRY SAUCE
1	5-OUNCE PACKAGE CHERRY GELATIN
1	15-OUNCE CAN PINEAPPLE, CRUSHED AND DRAINED (JUICE RESERVED)
1	CUP PECANS, CHOPPED
3	OUNCES CREAM CHEESE, SOFTENED

In a saucepan, combine water and cranberry sauce. While stirring, bring to a boil and continue boiling for 1 minute. Stir in gelatin, dissolving well. Remove from heat; add pineapple and nuts. Pour into a casserole dish and chill until set. Meanwhile, combine softened cream cheese and pineapple juice reserve. Spread on top of the set gelatin mixture. Yield: 6–8 servings.

Fig Pudding

1	CUP FRESH FIGS, MASHED
2	TEASPOONS BAKING SODA
$3/4$	CUP BROWN SUGAR
$3/4$	CUP GRANULATED SUGAR
$1/2$	CUP MARGARINE OR BUTTER, SOFTENED
2	EGGS
1	TABLESPOON LEMON JUICE
1	CUP ALL-PURPOSE FLOUR
1	TEASPOON CINNAMON
$1/2$	TEASPOON ALLSPICE
$1/2$	TEASPOON SALT
1	CUP WALNUT PIECES
$1/2$	CUP RAISINS

In a small bowl, combine figs and baking soda. Set aside. In a larger bowl, cream sugars and margarine or butter. Add the eggs and lemon juice, mixing well. Stir in the dry ingredients, walnuts, and raisins. Add the fig mixture and mix until well blended. Pour into a greased two-quart mold. Cover mold with foil. Meanwhile, fill a five-quart Dutch oven $2/3$ full of water or any pot large enough to hold the mold. (The mold needs to be elevated so that hot water can circulate underneath.) Put the mold inside the Dutch oven, cover, and steam for 2 hours on the stovetop on medium heat. Remove from water and cool for approximately 10 minutes. Invert pudding onto a serving dish. Serve warm with whipped topping if desired. Persimmons can be substituted for the figs. Yield: 12 servings.

Praline Pumpkin Custard

This recipe is contributed by Shirley Micelli.

12	PECAN HALVES
1	15-OUNCE CAN PUMPKIN
$2/3$	CUP WHOLE MILK
2	EGGS
$1/2$	TEASPOON BUTTERNUT VANILLA FLAVORING
1	TEASPOON PUMPKIN PIE SPICE
$1/2$	CUP GRANULATED SUGAR
	DASH OF SALT

Preheat oven to 350 degrees. Place pecan halves in the bottoms of 4 individual-sized greased custard dishes. Combine remaining ingredients, mixing well. Pour into custard dishes. Fill a baking dish half full of hot water. Set dishes in pan and bake 30 minutes or until set. Cool and invert. Serve with praline sauce and whipped topping if desired (see p. 120). Yield: 4 servings.

Favorite Ice Cream

$3/4$ CUP GRANULATED SUGAR
$1/2$ $1/4$-OUNCE ENVELOPE PLAIN GELATIN
2   CUPS WHOLE MILK, DIVIDED
1   EGG, SLIGHTLY BEATEN
2   CUPS CANNED EVAPORATED MILK
2   TEASPOONS VANILLA
   DASH OF SALT

In a saucepan, combine sugar, gelatin, and half the milk. Cook over low heat until gelatin dissolves. Stir a small amount of hot mixture into the beaten egg. Pour egg mixture back into the saucepan and continue cooking until slightly thickened. Chill. Stir in cream, vanilla, and salt. Freeze. Yield $1^1/_2$ quarts.

CHOCOLATE
Increase sugar to 1 cup. Add 6 ounces of chocolate chips in the saucepan at the beginning. Decrease vanilla to 1 teaspoon.

FRUIT
Decrease sugar to $1/2$ cup. Decrease vanilla to $1/2$ teaspoon. Add 2–3 cups fresh chopped or mashed fruit mixed with an additional $3/4$ cup of sugar to the chilled mixture.

It was a family tradition to meet Sunday evening after church for homemade ice cream and homemade desserts. Great-great-aunt Rena was an excellent baker, and the kids always looked forward to her dessert surprises. I hope all families have an Aunt Rena!

Appendix A
Cajun Cooking Glossary

Andouille Sausage—a pork sausage

Beignets—French doughnuts

Benne seeds—sesame seeds

Bisque—thick, creamy soup usually made of shellfish or crawfish

Boudin—a Cajun sausage made with rice, spices, and meats

Cajun cooking—a simple but pungent and robust type of cooking

Calas—a fried rice patty, usually dusted with confectioner's sugar

Cane Syrup—uniquely strong-flavored thick syrup that comes from sugar cane

Cayenne Pepper—red pepper; made from capsicum hot pepper

Chicory—a plant whose leaves are used in salads, and the root is ground and mixed with coffee

Courtboullion—a fish stew made with vegetables, seasonings, and sometimes wine

Coush Coush—a corn meal mush served for breakfast with milk and sugar

Creole cooking—a more elegant and spicier type of cooking, with peppers and usually tomatoes

Dirty Rice—a rice dish made with livers and giblets giving it a dirty appearance and wild taste

Étouffeé—to smother

Filé Powder—ground sassafras leaves

Fritters—a small fried cake or patty

Grits—coarsely ground dried hominy eaten mainly at breakfast

Gumbo—an African word meaning okra; a thick stew made with okra and many other ingredients

Jambalaya—this word originates from ham bone; a stew with rice and various meats

King Cake—the traditional Mardi Gras dessert

Maque Choux—an Indian fried corn dish

Pain Perdu—"Lost bread" or French toast

Praline—a candy made of brown sugar and nuts

Remoulade—a cold seafood dish served in a marinade of spices with salad dressing or mayonnaise

Roux—French for russet or reddish brown; a flour and oil mixture cooked to a russet color.

Sauce Piquant—a sauce with a sharp or piercing taste

Saute—to cook in fat. (This is the original Cajun meaning of the term. Modern cooks may understand this term to mean "to cook over high heat.")

The Cajun Cook's Pantry
(Necessary foods to have on hand for Cajun cooking.)

Bay leaves
Bell peppers
Brown sugar
Cayenne pepper
Celery
Coffee (strong)
Crab, fresh
Crawfish, fresh
Filé powder
Fish, fresh
Flour
Garlic
Green onion
Okra, fresh
Onion
Parsley, fresh
Pecans
Red hot sauce
Shrimp, fresh
Tomatoes, fresh
Vegetable oil
Worcestershire sauce
Yams or sweet potatoes, fresh

THE MODERN CAJUN COOK ADDS:
Cajun seasoning
Canned cream soups
Corn, frozen
Crab, canned
Okra, frozen
Packaged frozen crawfish tails
Parsley, dried
Prepared roux
Canned tomatoes with chili peppers
Seasoned bread crumbs

Appendix C
Measurements and Equivalents

Apples	1 medium	1 cup chopped
Bananas	1 medium	I cup sliced or $^2/_3$ cup mashed
Beans, dried	1 cup dried	2 cups cooked
Bell peppers	1 medium	1 cup chopped
Bread crumbs	2 slices	1 cup crumbs
Celery	1 rib	$^1/_3$ cup chopped
Cheese	4 ounces	1 cup grated
Chocolate chips	12 ounce bag	1 $^1/_2$ cups
Coffee	1 10-oz. package	140–160 cups or 70–80 cups strong Louisiana coffee
Confectioner's sugar	1 pound box	4 cups
Corn, fresh	1 large ear	1 cup kernels
Crabs, canned	6 ounce can	$^1/_2$ cup crabmeat
Crabs, fresh	6–8	1 cup crabmeat
Crawfish, fresh	5 pounds	1 pound tails
Eggplant	1 medium	5 cups chopped, 2 $^1/_2$ cups cooked and mashed
Figs, fresh	10 medium	1 cup chopped
Fish fillets	1 pound	3–4 average size fillets
Green onions	1 bunch	1 $^1/_2$ cups chopped
Grits	1 cup	1 $^1/_2$ cup cooked
Lemon	1 medium	2–3 tablespoons juice
Margarine or butter	1 stick	$^1/_2$ cup
Marshmallows	16 large	1 cup creme
Nut halves	4 ounce	Approximately 1 cup chopped
Okra, fresh	1 pound	2 $^1/_2$ cups sliced
Onions	1 small	$^1/_2$ cup chopped
	1 medium	1 cup chopped
	1 large	1 $^1/_2$ cups chopped
Orange	1 medium	$^1/_3$ cup juice
Parsley	1 tablespoon fresh	1 teaspoon dried
Pasta	2 ounces dried	1 cup cooked
Pears	1 medium	$^2/_3$ cup sliced
Potatoes	1 medium	$^2/_3$ cup chopped
Rice	1 cup uncooked	2 cups cooked
Shrimp	1 pound small	70–80 count
	1 pound medium	50–65 count
	1 pound large	30–45 count
Shrimp, chopped	8 ounces	1 cup chopped
Squash	1 pound	3–4 pieces
Sweet potatoes	1 pound	1 $^1/_4$ cups mashed
Tomatoes, fresh	1 medium	$^2/_3$ cup chopped
Yeast	1 packet	2 $^1/_4$ teaspoons powder
Zucchini	1 pound	3–4 pieces

Appendix D
Measurements and Weights

Dash	=	less than $1/4$ teaspoon
3 teaspoons	=	1 tablespoon
2 tablespoons	=	$1/8$ cup or 1 fluid ounce
4 tablespoons	=	$1/4$ cup
5 $1/3$ tablespoons	=	$1/3$ cup
8 tablespoons	=	$1/2$ cup
16 tablespoons	=	1 cup or 8 fluid ounces
2 cups	=	1 pint
4 cups	=	2 pints or 1 quart
2 pints	=	1 quart
4 quarts	=	1 gallon
8 quarts	=	1 peck
4 pecks	=	1 bushel
16 ounces	=	1 pound
1 ounce	=	28.35 grams
1 jigger	=	1–2 fluid ounces

Appendix E
Emergency Substitutions

Yeast, 1 package	2 $1/4$ teaspoons powder, or $1/3$ compressed cake
Baking powder, 1 teaspoon	$1/4$ baking soda plus $1/2$ cream of tartar
Cake flour, 1 cup	1 cup plus 2 tablespoons all-purpose flour
Self rising flour, 1 cup	1 cup all-purpose flour plus 1 $1/2$ teaspoons baking powder plus $1/2$ teaspoon salt
Cornstarch, 1 tablespoon	2 tablespoons all-purpose flour
Buttermilk, 1 cup	1 tablespoon vinegar or lemon juice plus enough whole milk to make 1 cup
Sour cream, 1 cup	1 cup plain yogurt
Half and half, 1 cup	$7/8$ cup whole milk plus 3 tablespoons margarine or butter
Lemon, 1 medium	2–3 tablespoons bottled lemon juice
Orange, 1 medium	$1/3$ cup orange juice
Semi-sweet chocolate, 1 ounce	1 ounce unsweetened plus 1 tablespoon granulated sugar or 3 tablespoons chocolate chips
Parsley, 1 tablespoon fresh	1 teaspoon dried
Herbs, 1 tablespoon fresh	1 teaspoon dried
Garlic, 1 clove	$1/8$ teaspoon powder
Onion, 1 small	1 tablespoon dehydrated
Whole milk, 1 cup	$1/2$ cup canned milk plus $1/2$ cup water

Index